Truth Decay

How Bitcoin Fixes This

Unveiling the Path to Financial Freedom

Victoria Collette Jones

For Lucy…

Here for only three days, forever in our hearts.

CONTENTS

"That's not fair,"
        said the child.
"Life isn't fair,"
        said the parent.
"That's wrong,"
        said the inner child,
"We should at least try to make it fair!"

"What is fair?"
        said the World.

INTRODUCTION

MODERN TECHNOLOGY HAS burst into our lives, giving us unprecedented access to more information than we have ever had before. In addition to this information we are bombarded with more varied opinions than we have ever known before. Our minds and our ideas are rapidly changing. Some of this new knowledge is helpful. Some of what we learn is misleading. Some material is downright lies. It can lead us down paths we never would have journeyed down otherwise.

What we learn provides the foundation for what we believe, and these beliefs are extremely powerful. From religion to science to propaganda, these beliefs influence who we love and who we hate, the sacrifices we are prepared to make, the things we wish to build, and what we are prepared to say no to. When an outcome does not align with what we believe should happen, it can send us to the depths of despair. Sometimes this despair can rapidly dissipate when we are introduced to a new piece of information that dramatically changes our perspective.

Our beliefs also manage our society. They influence the politicians we support and these politicians in turn are responsible for the rules and laws they make for our society. The only influence we have to affect these laws (unless we put effort into campaigning or fundraising, which may or may not be effective) is who we believe we should vote for.

Now we have computers. These computers allow someone to program in a series of rules and operate in a way so that no one else can change them. Increasingly, the use of these computers is having a substantial impact on how our society progresses. Is this a good thing? Maybe, if we use the right rules. But what are the right rules? Have we reached a point in society where we have become so out of tune with what reasonable rules are that we are in danger of programming in all the wrong ones?

What if these rules relate to our money?

I recently met with a friend who had made the decision to take control of her pension. She was worried about how things were looking in the financial markets. For many months she studied to understand the rules for Small Self-Administered Pension Schemes in the UK and completed all the paperwork. Then the government changed the rules through the Financial Conduct Authority. Effectively saying to her and anyone else wanting to follow a similar strategy—you can't do that anymore!

What are the outcomes for society when the rules of the law conflict with the rules of the heart?

If a heart says,

"I want to be prosperous, successful and protect my future," but the law says,

"No, you can't do it that way!"

We live in a world with rules crowding in on us from every angle. It is becoming suffocating. When all avenues to freedom close off, where do we go and what do we do? How did we even end up here?

These are very important questions, the outcomes of which will have serious consequences. Are we aware enough and informed enough to make the choices that will make our future a happy, successful, and prosperous one? Or are we headed down a dark and foreboding path, a digital prison from which all chances of escape are lost?

Technology in itself is neutral. It is how we use it that will make all the difference. A rule that is good for one person can be very bad for another, leading to unfortunate unintended consequences for many. For this reason they need to be considered very carefully.

From my own perspective, I believe that the rules programmed into Bitcoin, as a new technology, are taking us closer to the better path. That is why I have chosen to focus on Bitcoin here.

This book started as a "how-to" book that explained to business owners how to accept bitcoin payments in their business. Attempting this in my own dental business gave me some important insights that I felt I could share with others. Then, as the book evolved, I realized that there is so much more to the story. Accepting payment in bitcoin is the easy part. Understanding why you should is another story entirely.

In the lead-up to writing this book, I spent time in the Bitcoin community, making friends at conferences, getting acquainted with some well-known names, and learning more about the technology and its history. The story of how the technology of Bitcoin came into being is interesting in itself. The belief system that keeps the technology going is a revelation.

I find the tale fascinating. As I have experience running my own business and insight into working in health care, public and private, I decided to include my personal journey with Bitcoin—how I became interested in it and what motivated me to take a serious look at the technology. As part of this story I have gone to some lengths to explain how the financial system currently works and the effect that this is having on our legal system and on our welfare system.

To help structure the information, the first section of the book is titled "Why?—The Past". This is the story that led me to my interest in Bitcoin. The second section is titled "How?—The Present". This goes into the technology of Bitcoin more deeply, showing you how to accept bitcoin as payment in your business. It also outlines why you would want to do this. The third section, titled "When?—The Future", discusses the implications for a future based on Bitcoin and other blockchain technologies.

This book is not designed for traders or speculators, nor for those wanting a deep analysis of the Bitcoin technology, although these groups are still likely to find my story interesting. My main aim is to give you a clearer idea of the features and benefits behind Bitcoin. For those of you currently unfamiliar with Bitcoin, I want you to have the ability to accept Bitcoin payments, either as an individual or a business, immediately when the need arises, and to understand the implications of doing so. In a crisis, you will need this information quickly and in a digestible style.

This book features many ideas on the financial system, politics, and the law. I use my own personal story to make these topics more relatable and easier to understand. My aim is to provide you with an overall picture, the essential elements of what I believe it would most benefit you to know.

This is a rapidly changing area of study—new technological developments are occurring all the time. Some ideas that are new to you may require you to do further research. There are many sources of information available, but few that tie everything together. This book aims to provide that summary, to furnish you with more clarity on where the world is likely to be going in the future, and in doing so, instruct you on how you can regain some control in a situation of ever-increasing financial strife.

With the economic system teetering, it is wise to be prepared. This book is designed to assist you in this. If you think everything is just fine—you really need to read this book!

For more information about me and the way I can help you
and others learn more about Bitcoin,
please visit my website at
www.satoshispage.com.

WHY?
The Past

CHAPTER ONE

The Beginning…

I WAS FIFTEEN years old and all I could hear was a low groan coming from the upstairs bathroom. Shifting my weight from right to left, I hovered at the top of the landing. It is a terrible thing to hear someone you love suffering, and not know what to do.

My father was still at work and my five siblings were downstairs. I was now home from school and my mother was in labor with her seventh child.

Four hours later, as the drama unfolded upstairs, the entire Local Health Authority appeared to have arrived at our house: three doctors, six nurses, and five emergency medical responders. I watched as they came downstairs and carried a scrawny little bundle out of the front door.

Lucy—my little sister.

That was the last time I saw her. Three days later, she died.

My mother developed diabetes during her pregnancy. As a result, her doctor insisted that she was high-risk and must go to the hospital for a caesarean section, as she had before with her sixth baby. My mother—who had a terrible birthing experience with her sixth baby but a very straightforward time with her third, fourth, and fifth— refused. The thought of a repeat experience of the last birth filled her with terror.

Her doctor, in his efforts to persuade my mother to do what he believed was the right thing (or what the NHS [UK National Health Service] demanded of him), cajoled, threatened, and finally struck her off his register, massively increasing her anxiety. Because she refused to cooperate. It was a holy mess.

My mother acted as responsibly as she felt she could, while staying true to what she felt was right. She researched the issue. In doing this she discovered that there were plenty of other women who had managed a natural birth after a previous caesarean section. She diligently followed the instructions she had been given to manage her diabetic condition, stabbing her finger every morning to keep an eye on her blood sugars and adjusting her diet.

The result was as it was, however. Almost everyone blamed my mother for ignoring the doctors and thinking she knew best. It was heartbreaking. The distress forever etched in my mind, after the event, by watching a solitary tear roll down my father's left cheek as they said prayers for our family at the local church.

My mother was thirty-six by the time she had her seventh child. She was told about all the dire consequences of her actions, including the possibility that the child could be handicapped. My mother's philosophy, in spite of her anxiety, was that nature has a way of taking care of these things. Interference would likely make things worse. Nature should be allowed to run its course.

In this case it did. I still wonder, though, if a kinder, more understanding attitude from the medical profession, rather than a dictatorial one, might have helped the situation.

So began my perplexing observation of our society.

I considered a career as a doctor. But I didn't have the stomach for these life-and-death dilemmas. At the time there were constant reports in the newspapers of how young doctors were working such long shifts that they hardly got any sleep. As a teenager, I really valued my sleep. Medicine clearly wasn't for me.

I became a dentist instead.

You may think it is unusual for a dentist to be writing a book about Bitcoin. But there are particular reasons why my career and interests have led me to this point in history.

Let me begin.

As I was growing up, my father was a naval officer. So I was given the opportunity to go to a private convent boarding school for two and a half years at the age of twelve. I loved this school. But the school had to close after the stock market crash of 1987—the first example of how a financial crisis would affect my life. So my secondary education was completed at the local comprehensive school instead. I then studied for my A-levels at the local tertiary college.

There were a wide range of careers that I could have chosen at the age of sixteen. Yet my choices were mainly influenced by the things that surrounded me at the time. When I went to the dentist, I was impressed by the environment. What amazed me even more was that my father, who always seemed to struggle to pay for everything, had no problem sending us into this space-age environment to have our teeth checked. Because, for some reason, this service was free.

It seemed like it would be fun to spend my days playing with futuristic equipment and helping people at the same time. I had a very clear idea of what I thought I would achieve by choosing this profession: grateful patients and beautiful smiles. This contrasted, however, with what I saw as I looked around me. If this sophisticated service was available for free, how come there were so many people who had teeth that looked bad, whereas the Americans seemed to be well-known for their white, sparkly, bright smiles? There was a mismatch here that I didn't fully understand until many years later, after I had spent much time studying the impact of politics, finance, and the law on the subject of health care.

In 1992 I set off for university, full of wide-eyed dreams, full of joy and wonder at the sophisticated career that I was entering. It wasn't long before reality kicked in. I became more and more disappointed. Being a dentist is hard. It isn't just intellectually challenging, because the system has been made so convoluted; it is physically and emotionally challenging. I remember my first day on the clinic floor, dressed in my white coat with a mask around my face and gloves on my hands. Discovering that my nose was itchy and I was unable to touch it.

"This is my very definition of hell," I thought to myself, but there was no going back now.

It turns out that, unlike most of my friends and family, a large majority of society appears to hate the dentist. I even had a dentist friend who kept a tally chart behind the door of his office when he first graduated, so that when someone came in and said "I hate the dentist!", he would put a tick on the tally chart and say "Excellent—you are the fifth one today!" He was clearly able to cope with this better than I was.

Having now spent many years in the dental profession, I think much of this attitude is down to how powerless people feel when subjected to the dictates of an authoritarian profession, similar to the experience of my mother with the medics. With life itself apparently dependent on these unsympathetic authority figures that can cause you pain, I would be inclined to hate them too, especially if I had a history of appalling experiences, which—as I have sadly learned from speaking with them—many of my patients have had.

I had very limited comprehension of this when I decided to become a dentist at the beginning of my journey. I studied well at university and learned to be the best dentist that I could. I was fortunate that I trained in London and received one of the most outstanding educations in the world, available at that time, to become a dentist. Five years of being a student took a big toll on my finances, though, because I had to fund myself through the process. Even though university fees didn't need to be paid by students while they were in school, after not earning anything for five years and still having to pay my living expenses, I was £60,000 in debt by the time I graduated.

It is only now that I understand more about finance, and the way in which the financial system works, that I fully realize what a burden this was at the time. My parents used to joke that they brought all of us up on credit cards. The immediate moment was what I was taught to consider. Compound interest? I had no clue.

Graduating was a huge relief. I was now free to go out into the world to earn a living. But then, of course, my understanding of how the world worked was still only just beginning.

Through the 1970s and 1980s, dentistry in the UK had been provided, in the main, through the government-funded National Health Service (NHS). But in 1992, just as I decided that I wanted to enter this esteemed profession, the government made the decision to cut the fees they would pay dentists. So by the time I qualified in 1997, private dentistry was starting to emerge as a legitimate career option, as dentists increasingly rejected their NHS contracts and sought to regain some control over their future.

As I entered the profession this drama was playing out and is still ongoing today: a constant—and very tiresome—seesaw and debate over what the dentists want compared to what the government believes they should have. I left the drama behind and moved into the private sector, where I could provide my patients with what I felt they really needed, as soon as I could. This meant they would have to pay more for my services—often significantly more—than they would have to pay if they had received the same item of service on the NHS.

This was problematic. Private dentistry was only just beginning to gain a foothold in the UK. Finding a good place to work, with a business model that balanced what I wanted to deliver as a dentist with adequate financial compensation, was tricky. I worked for small family businesses. I worked for large chains of dental practices. I hoped they would have better management models and goals. Sometimes they did, sometimes they didn't. For a while, I had to take a hiatus and go back to working for the NHS. This lasted a very short time before I was starting to look for a way out again.

In spite of the difficulties, I experienced quite a varied and interesting career over the first ten years. But eventually, I no longer felt satisfied working as an associate dentist for someone else. Nowhere that I had worked had allowed me to deliver the dentistry I wanted to deliver in a satisfactory way. Although I had never intended to run my own business, I finally reached the stage where I realized that was the only way that I could deliver the dentistry that I wanted.

I found a small room inside a smart hairdressing salon that looked like it would suit my purposes as a place to start. Establishing the legal agreement was very trying, however. The agreement was not just going to be with the hairdressers, but also with their landlords. Negotiating the lease took eighteen exhausting months. By this stage, I was eight months pregnant with my first child, wondering whether I should give up on the whole thing. It certainly felt like the whole universe was conspiring to stop me in my tracks. Little did I know the dramas that were unfolding behind the scenes in the financial system.

I had seen the long queues outside of the Northern Rock Building Society in the summer of 2007, but I was completely clueless as to what was going on. All I was really interested in was finding a way in which I could work in peace and have things under my own control. I wanted to provide the best service that I could to my patients and pay my bills with a degree of consistency.

Finally, by December 2007, my little business was open, and my daughter was born in February 2008. Everyone thought I was mad.

To me, however, having worked for a number of private dental businesses from their opening, I understood that it would be quiet in the beginning. I knew that I had the ability to build my client list and a successful business regardless of the circumstances, and in the end that is what I did.

What I had not bargained for was the financial crisis of 2008. As a dentist, I had never had any problems at all with borrowing money from the bank. In fact, this had been part of my contingency plan when I started my business. I had a small amount of savings, but most of the business, the equipment, and materials were funded through lease agreements over five years at a range of 11 to 15 percent interest rates. I didn't really look too closely at this at the time. I didn't anticipate money being a problem, I just wanted to get the business up and running.

September 15, 2008, was the last time I received a loan from a bank. Although I desperately needed one after that and applied many times, I could not get one anywhere. For me, this was exceptionally bad timing. Nine months into my business, my savings depleted, I was exhausted from trying to run a business and look after my new baby. And I suddenly found myself more strapped for cash than I had ever been in my life.

In the end, the only way the business survived was because I was able to continue to pay for the expenses of the business by using my credit cards and moving the balances to a new credit card offer until I had used up the maximum limits on all of them. This bought me another year. Although things were improving and the outlook of the business was brighter, my cash flow was extremely tight. There were days when, if something had gone wrong with an individual patient's treatment and I had been unable to charge them for my work that day, I would have been bankrupt the following week. It was a very stressful state of affairs, but by some miracle I survived.

Eventually, things started to get easier and I could breathe again. I was able to take on a business coach who helped me make the business more productive. But I never wanted to be in that situation ever again.

It is sometimes hard for others to appreciate, I think, exactly what goes on behind the scenes of some businesses. Imagine, if you will, a busy day in a dental office. Nervous patients. Explaining complicated treatment and plans. Delivering tricky treatment procedures. Managing equipment. Negotiating with engineers, suppliers, landlords, staff, banks, and credit card companies. I could go on. In the midst of all this, the dental nurse arrives in the operating room to announce that the card machine isn't working again. This was one of the most frustrating aspects of my life at the time.

Clients were charged for each item of treatment as it was completed. If the client left without paying this would affect the cash flow of the business. Most of the time we knew the patients and they were very understanding. But sometimes we didn't. When the card machine played up, we had to ask clients to go down the road to withdraw some additional cash, because usually we were charging for treatment above and beyond what most people were carrying around at the time.

One of the other issues that we encountered were glitches in the operation of the banks. It only happened a couple of times, but it was enough to stimulate my thinking on such matters. Before I owned my own business I didn't really understand how things like card machines worked. I had never needed to know.

It turns out there are companies that manage the acceptance of payments through a card machine. It is then the bank's task to transfer this money to the business's bank account, usually within a few days. If there is a problem with the banking intermediary, this directly affects the business. At the time there were reports in the news of people not getting their wages on time, direct debits not being processed, and all sorts of other issues. In my particular case, when the banks were having problems, any payments I had taken that day wound up being delayed, beyond the normal time delay, by an additional period of three to five days.

Fortunately, by this time my cash flow issues were mostly resolved, so I was able to handle this blip. But if this had happened at a different stage in my business development, it would clearly have been a serious crisis to deal with. Happily, I was able to analyze the situation much more calmly. I reflected on the vulnerabilities within the financial system. I concluded that if there were ever a problem with the cash flowing through the business, due to problems with the banks, there was the potential that my business would not survive. It was this conclusion that first made me look for alternatives.

I recall hearing about Bitcoin fairly early. It was mentioned in the news occasionally at first, and then began to be featured heavily in media coverage when the price was increasing exponentially in 2013. I saw a clip of a Netflix series called *The Good Wife* where Bitcoin was mentioned. I wasn't strongly motivated to research it, but it was definitely within my consciousness. I knew that it existed.

By 2015 I finally managed to sell a house I had been trying to sell for seven years. For the first time in a long time, I had some money I could save. This was a very precious thing to me and I wanted to make sure that I looked after it as well as I could. By this time interest rates were becoming ridiculously low. I was also conscious of the concept of inflation, the way in which prices continually tend to creep up. I knew that it was important that I had some kind of inflation protection for my savings.

So I started learning about money.

I went to see a financial adviser who showed me a chart demonstrating the exponential rise of the stock market. I was skeptical—I had heard that my maternal grandmother was generously well-provided for by her late husband when she was widowed, but then lost it all after receiving bad financial advice.

"What happens if the stock market crashes?" I asked.

"You DON'T sell," came the reply.

"Good grief," I thought.

Anything that has done nothing but rise for one hundred years with only the occasional blip seems suspicious to me. There was something not quite right here. So I started to learn more about money. How money is debt. The difference between Keynesian economics and Austrian economics. This eventually led me to the concept of sound money—money that preserves its value—and the historical importance of gold and silver in this role.

I realized that as a business I was never going to be keen on accepting gold and silver coins in exchange for my services. It was hard enough getting to the bank to deposit cash, let alone bags of metal. Not to mention the difficulties in establishing whether the gold and silver offered was genuine. Clearly, this was not going to be the future for business transactions. So at this point, I was looking for something else.

Where was the digital solution?

It was already there in the back of my mind.

It was Bitcoin.

CHAPTER TWO

Money

IN THE SUMMER of 2017, I was sitting in a pub in Reading. It was a sunny day and I was fortunate to meet up with my sister Charlotte. Like me, she had recently decided that a career change was in order, and so for a brief period our time was our own. I was in Reading for a course, while she already lived there, and we had escaped to the pub for the afternoon to catch up. Now Charlotte is not unintelligent. Educated to masters level, with some years working for the Serious Fraud Office, it is possible for her to grasp a concept. Yet, when talking to her about Bitcoin, it was clear that she had no idea how money works.

"What do you think gives money its value?" I asked.

"Our pound notes represent the amount of gold in the bank," she replied rather scornfully.

I laughed.

"No, Charlotte, they don't," I said. "Our pound notes haven't represented an amount of gold in the bank since 1931, and no country on Earth has had a currency that represents gold since 1971, when Richard Nixon took the US dollar off the gold standard!"

A surprising number of people still believe that our money continues to operate on a gold standard. A recent study showed that 29 percent of Americans currently believe this.[1]

The truth of the matter right now is that our money is actually debt. Take a look at an English twenty-pound note and under the name "Bank of England" you will see the words, "I promise to pay the bearer on demand the sum of twenty pounds."

"Twenty pounds of what?" you may ask.

The same applies to other currencies around the world. On the US dollar you will see the words "Federal Reserve Note," and similar to the Bank of England, this is a promise from the central bank to make a payment to you—but a payment of what?

These notes are essentially debt, promises from the central bank to pay you, and anyone else that holds them, a certain amount of money. They began by representing an amount of gold held by the bank, but gradually, mainly due to the expense of wars over the last century, creative accounting behind the scenes has made them essentially worth less and less.

---

1   https://www.prnewswire.com/news-releases/new-genesis-mining-study-finds-29-of-americans-believe-the-us-dollar-is-still-backed-by-gold-300947883.html

This can be seen in the way that prices are gradually creeping up and the size or quantity of the products we buy is gradually going down—a phenomenon known as "shrinkflation." Similarly, as I witnessed while working in the dental profession for the NHS, the quality of the service we receive is also getting worse and worse.

When I talk to my friends about the problems in the financial system, one of the best examples I use to illustrate my point is the growth in property prices that we have experienced, particularly in the past forty years. There was a time when property was not an attractive investment purely because of the costs of ongoing maintenance. Ownership of property would often be seen as more of a cost than an asset.

In the past forty years, however, the population has been conditioned to believe that the ownership of property is the equivalent of, and will operate in parallel to, your savings in a bank account. Pay off the first mortgage you had twenty years ago and now you have an asset against which you can take out another loan. You will still have another twenty years left in the workforce, most likely, so potentially by taking out another mortgage you can give yourself an attractive bonus with which you are immediately able to elevate your quality of life.

Yes, in recent times property has been an excellent investment, but this, I explain to my friends, is not because property is becoming more valuable. It is because our money is becoming less valuable. In a situation where money itself is constantly losing purchasing power, to preserve your wealth it is wise to buy an asset where the value is maintained. The quality of our money is now deteriorating all the time—it is not tied to anything solid anymore.

So how did we get here?

The can of worms with our money was opened after the First and Second World Wars in the first half of the twentieth century.

As has happened throughout history, it is the desire of governments or leaders to go to war, or spend lavishly, that is usually the beginning of a currency problem. In ancient Rome, as new lands to conquer started to dwindle, Nero began clipping coins and devaluing them by mixing them with baser metals to continue to fund price controls and lavish lifestyles in the city. This eventually led to the fall of the Roman Empire.

In more modern times, by the beginning of the twentieth century, Europe had experienced fifty years of prosperity with most of the countries in Europe on a gold standard. The citizens had become complacent, trusting the banknotes that stipulated that they were worth an equivalent amount of gold held in the banks' vaults. As can often happen, being prosperous for too long can make people fail to consider, or forget outright, the troubles of the past.

With the outbreak of war, astronomical expenses began to pile up across Europe, triggering a looming financial disaster. Under a gold standard, this catastrophe would have been limited; because it is difficult and expensive to create more gold, the only way to fund a war under a gold standard is to tax the citizens of the country involved. Instead, European countries resorted to a new tactic: some clever accounting which stipulated that the notes issued by the bank were temporarily no longer convertible to gold.

As such, the snowball effect of fiat currency—currency by decree rather than inherent value—began. Hardly anyone batted an eyelid.

The First World War piled up ever-increasing expenses along with the equivalent destruction and death toll, the horror of which had never been seen before. Finally, once it was over, it was time to redress the finances.

In the 1930s the Great Depression occurred due to failed attempts at re-establishing a gold standard.[2] The price of gold was kept too low in comparison to the increased creation of notes from the war. This was done to try to control prices and prevent a recession by controlling deflation. Unfortunately the result was that this kept wages too high, businesses could no longer afford to employ the same number of workers, and by laying them off created massive unemployment.

As a solution, John Maynard Keynes, a prominent economist at the time, argued that money needed to be supplied to the economy to get it moving again. This would stimulate people to spend (aggregate demand), thereby increasing production and employing more workers.

There are those who argue that this approach, even though it is still in use today, is fundamentally flawed. For the everyday person this is hard to understand, so I share this analogy to make it more relatable.

Many people in the West are familiar with the popular board game Monopoly. The players try to win by moving around the board, buying and selling property, collecting a salary, and aiming to be the most profitable property owner. The game normally ends with most of the players running out of money because the winner has built up a solid property portfolio and the other players have to pay rent to them too many times. In the game of Monopoly the value of the money

---

2   *The Bitcoin Standard,* by Saifedean Ammous

is fixed and the prices of the properties are always the same, because the amount of money available and the prices of the properties are in balance in order to support the game. The mortgage interest rates are set at a particular level and the salary collected as you pass Go is always the same, £200. This is similar to (but not exactly like) how an economy works on a gold standard. The game is won by the skill of the players and the individual decisions they make in order to deploy their resources. In addition to a little luck.

The game feels unfair to the losers, however, because when the winner appears to have acquired all of the assets and is in the process of collecting rents, the bank has run out of money and there is nothing left for them. This is not what happens in the real economy because the chances are that the owner of, say, the hotel in Mayfair may employ the tenant who lives at Old Kent Road to come and do some repair work. This tenant would never consider staying at a hotel in Mayfair in a million years, so there is no danger of losing his savings that way. So the analogy has its limits—however, let's stay with it a little longer.

Some years ago Monopoly adapted the rules to stipulate that when the bank has run out of the money supplied by the game, you can use pieces of paper to create new notes to keep the game going. Anyone who has ever played this extended game of Monopoly knows that once you do this, it doesn't really improve anything. The players who have already acquired the most property retain an advantage, and the rest of the players receiving more money via the bank just wind up paying them more rent. The existing property owners get the opportunity to buy even more property and the rest of the players get to pay them even more rent. Receiving the extra money from the bank just prolongs the agony of ending the game, before some weary participant then suggests it might be better just to start again.

In 1936 the idea of injecting more money into the real economy was an attractive prospect for capitalist governments around the world. Buying into Keynes's ideas, they managed to avoid re-valuing gold and thereby deflating the assets of the wealthy. In the end, however, the only aggregate demand that lifted countries out of the Great Depression was another round of destruction, death, and massive spending: the Second World War, which once again created significant debt for the countries involved and compounded the problem.

In the real world, increasing the money supply as suggested by Keynes is achieved by creating more debt. A government can issue bonds (a guaranteed future payment by the government), lending them into the economy to investors in order to create the debt. The idea is that they can then reduce the debt by paying these bonds off with increased taxes when conditions improve. The only trouble is, the paying it back bit never seems to happen…

In 1944 so many countries were in debt after these terribly expensive wars that a new way needed to be found to manage their distorted currencies so that they could continue to trade with each other. So it was agreed at the Bretton Woods Conference that all of the other countries would now value their currencies against the US dollar. The dollar was still able to operate on a gold standard, as the US had been the main lender to the European countries fighting during the war, so most of these countries now owed them money. This came to an end in what is known as the "Nixon shock" of 1971, however, when Richard Nixon announced that America would no longer be honoring convertibility of the US dollar to gold.

Nowhere on Earth was money now used that sustained its value. Finance from this point on would only rely on the "rules" and the way in which certain central entities felt currencies should be managed. These rules were now dictated by governments and central banks such as the Bank for International Settlements (BIS), the International Monetary Fund (IMF), the Federal Reserve Bank in the US, the European Central Bank, and the Bank of England.

These rules had already created an explosion of economic science and theory, but after 1971 there was an equivalent explosion in government and banking intervention in order to manage it all. Notable names such as John Maynard Keynes, Friedrich Hayek, and Milton Friedman all had a part to play in advancing their theories in order to help manage this new world. Their attempts were for naught, however; in spite of it all, the world's debt mountain continued to balloon.

The result is that the world now has a credit card where no one ever comes to collect on the debt. World debt at the end of 2018 stood at $244 trillion.[3] One trillion dollars is a staggering number, a number that is bigger than most people can imagine. Take a look at some of the videos on YouTube designed to help you visualize a trillion dollars. If you spent one million dollars every day, from the day Jesus Christ was born until the end of 2019, you still would not have spent one trillion dollars—and that is just one trillion, let alone 244 of them!

---

3   https://www.bloomberg.com/news/articles/2019-01-15/global-debt-of-244-trillion-nears-record-despite-faster-growth

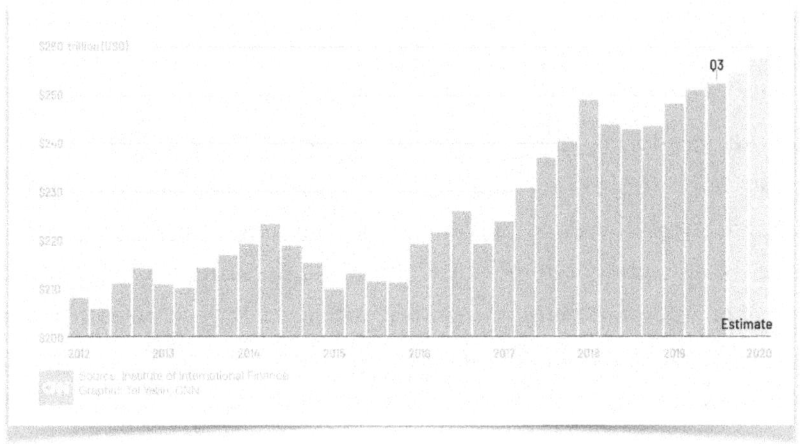

Global debt is now at record levels and rising quickly.

There are those that suggest that maybe the debt should now just be written off, but what one needs to realize, in our current magical money system, is that one entity's debt is another entity's assets. Assets held in the stock market, housing, and people's pensions. Pension funds buy these government bonds as a "safe" asset because they believe that governments have a reliable ability to tax their citizens. So writing off the debt, or even trying to deflate the debt, tends to cause significant problems as it diminishes the value of assets. In all of the financial crises of the past century, whether it be the Great Depression, the 1987 stock market crash, Japan's Lost Decade, or the 2008 financial crisis, the solution has always been the same: fudge the numbers and create more debt. This is a party that cannot continue forever.

History tells us that it will not go on forever. Typically fiat currencies have a forty-to-seventy-year life span before they collapse, taking their societies with them. Examples include the Roman Empire and Weimar Germany, and more recently Zimbabwe and Venezuela.

Our computers (which are relatively new) now allow markets to use sophisticated techniques to manage the prices of assets and interest rates. These manipulations are facilitated by stable Western governments that often collude with the banks, turning a blind eye on their activities and bailing them out whenever they get into trouble. All of this may have kept the game going longer than anyone ever expected. It may well go on a bit longer, but eventually it will end, because the game only lasts as long as everyone believes nothing will ever change.

Some imagine that nothing will ever change, because with every crisis that they have known so far in their lifetimes a solution has always been found. Same old, same old—we are destined to be in this cycle forever. But what if we aren't? What if, instead of allowing central banks to control our destinies, we had a digital gold equivalent that enabled us to start transacting honestly again, between each other in a way that required no third party? Something that sustained its quality because no one could create more of it out of thin air and deflate its value?

Understanding value is important. When we used to transact in gold everyone had a collective understanding of what the value of one ounce of gold was, and what we could buy with it. Creating more gold is very difficult and expensive, making it troublesome to increase the supply. As a result this keeps the value of the money stable.

Having money that is stable in value makes it possible for society to operate with a consistent understanding. This consistency allows us to make decisions in our daily lives because we are able to compare value easily and manage our finances.

If we save some of our gold rather than spending it, we are able to spend that gold in the future knowing it would still have the same value. We would be able to predict accurately what we could buy with it then.

Nowadays, because our money boils down to a set of rules, we need a degree in finance to make any headway in understanding the value of our money. Our only option, if we are to have any chance of prospering, is to hire someone else who has a degree in finance to help us manage our finances, like a financial adviser. Anyone who cannot access this resource is in serious trouble, because their only other option is to rely on the government to support them in their old age or any other situation where they could be financially vulnerable. Succeeding financially has become so complex the average person almost has no chance. Working hard and saving money doesn't work because the value of what you are able to save is constantly being lost due to the increasing money supply behind the scenes. Thus your ability to protect yourself from that is diminishing more and more rapidly.

This has consequences in society that are known as moral hazards, because when our money is no longer honest, our agreements are no longer honest. Inequality these days is no longer about who owns more money, as the value of this is now constantly changing. It is effectively more about the interest rates you are able to access at a particular moment in time.

If a worker earns their wages and is taxed at 30 percent before they can spend it, but a company can take on debt in order to repurchase their shares (ownership of their business) and simultaneously lower their tax bill to zero—this is a dishonest and unequal situation. Governments and corporations can operate at completely different levels financially because they can afford expert help when it comes to managing or manipulating their finances.

Governments can access negative interest rates, which in reality means they are being paid to borrow money, whereas the most impoverished in society are lucky if they can access a payday loan at a 300 percent rate! Corporations that need large amounts of debt can access cheap loans at perhaps 1 percent, well under the government's target inflation rate of 2 percent, whereas I as a new business owner with a ten-year track record as a professional was still only able to access lease agreements over five years at rates of 11–15 percent to start my little business. Hardly a fair playing field.

The same problem also applies to taxes: the more resources you have, the better access you have to financial professionals who can help you reduce your tax bill. The ultimate irony. The more debt you have, the less you have to pay.

We now have unicorn businesses such as Amazon, Facebook, Uber, and WeWork, whose objective is to acquire as much investment/debt as possible in order to grow as fast as possible, in order to dominate their particular market. By doing this and remaining unprofitable for many years, it also allows them to delay their tax bills for many years, and in the process they unfairly compete with all of the smaller businesses that cannot access those resources. Ultimately the smaller businesses fail, leaving the unicorn businesses as the only operator in that sector.

This is a strategy that I also witnessed and was a part of in the dentistry profession. As many of the smaller family operations struggled to continue to operate, the larger chains increased their portfolios by buying the smaller businesses. Their larger budgets allowed them to compete more efficiently. By having access to economies of scale they are more easily able to manage the increasing legislative burden and other costs placed on the profession by the government.

Yes, our money is a problem. It is even more complex than I have tried to outline here, and that complexity is partly what makes our lives so confusing. The ability of the average person to judge what is fair has been lost due to the loss of character in our money, and as a result everyone suffers. Individually we may operate in life in a way that we believe is fair, but eventually, due to distortions in the system within which we transact, we come up against obstacles that flummox us.

I have come up against a number of these obstacles in my quest to be the best dentist, and the fairest businessperson, that I could be. There are many business gurus that will tell you that it is possible to overcome any challenge, you just need to apply yourself more or use their technique and you will finally be successful. But what if the system is literally stacked against you?

I have listened to these gurus and bought into some of their ideas, and for a time they did work, but before long I would find myself up against the next roadblock. Finally I realized the true problem underneath all of these challenges: a rules-based system of money, set up by our forefathers to try to overcome the financial implications of irresponsible and unfettered war. And while many ended up paying one price for our freedom, dying in trenches far from home, their grandchildren and great grandchildren will be paying another price entirely.

CHAPTER THREE

Satoshi and the Rise of Bitcoin

IN EARLY 2009, in the shadows of the 2008 financial crisis, an anonymous software developer engaged with a well-known group of cyberpunks. He released his ideas to the group in a white paper titled "Bitcoin: A Peer-to-Peer Electronic Cash System." The first block of bitcoins were mined (to be explained later). Embedded in the first block he wrote the text:

> "The Times 03/Jan/2009 Chancellor on Brink of Second Bailout for Banks."

The name of the author was Satoshi Nakamoto. To this day no one knows who Satoshi is.

So began the phenomenon that has become Bitcoin, the best-performing asset of the recent decade. A single bitcoin's value has gone from less than a cent in 2010 to just under $20,000 in 2017. To what does Bitcoin owe this magic, and why is it still one of the most undervalued assets on the planet, in comparison to world debt, with a current market cap (total value) of just under $168 billion?

Bitcoin was not the first digital currency. A number of attempts had been made to create a digital currency before Satoshi's Bitcoin. In 1983 a research paper by David Chaum introduced the idea of digital cash using public-key and private-key cryptography. In 1990 he founded Digicash, an electronic cash company, in Amsterdam to commercialize the ideas in his research. Chaum eventually maintained that the Digicash project entered the market before e-commerce was fully integrated within the internet and thereby stunted its growth. Digicash filed for bankruptcy in 1998 and sold its assets in 2002.

Milton Friedman, the prominent economist, discussed in the 1990s how a form of internet money was required to reach the true potential of the internet. Interestingly, at the same time, he also predicted that this new internet money would be one of the major forces in reducing the role of government around the world.

E-gold was the first widely used internet money. Introduced in 1996, it allowed transactions for an equivalent amount of gold, and developed a system that allowed for payments (including micropayments) worldwide. It grew to several million users before the US government shut it down in 2008, citing problems with user identification and the failure to cut off illegal and abusive activity in its user community. While this might have seemed entirely reasonable from the US government's point of view, it demonstrated to the cyberworld the dangers of inventing a new form of money with centralized control: the owner is exposed and can be targeted by a more powerful adversary.

Our current fiat money—dollars, pounds, euros, and the like—through their rules of operation, rely for their management on governments and central banks. Not only this, but the ability of governments to manage their currency through the laws they make gives them a great deal of power. Any kind of independent money is a direct threat to them, so while problems with identification and failure to cut off abusive activity may be given as reasons to shut down a new form of currency, the real reason may be entirely different.

Perhaps understanding the vulnerability of implementers of dangerous new ideas, Satoshi chose to keep himself anonymous. Indeed, since Bitcoin's inception there have been numerous stories of home raids and arrests of people who may possibly be Satoshi. The most famous among them was Dorian Prentice Satoshi Nakamoto, an innocent Californian engineer who just so happens to share the same name as the infamous Bitcoin creator.

The name Satoshi in Japanese means "intelligent history" or "clear thinking, quick-witted, and wise," while the name "Nakamoto" means "central origin" or "one who lives in the middle," as Japanese people with this surname came mainly from the central trading hub of Japan. The use of the moniker "Satoshi Nakamoto" to identify the author of the new technology in the Bitcoin white paper suggests that the choice of the name was deliberate. I have sometimes wondered whether the choice of a Japanese name was a nod to the Japanese people who appear to have suffered greatly as a result of increased debt, enduring decades of stagflation since the 1990s. The implication is that they have the most to gain by choosing to start transacting and saving in a new digital form of sound money.

By inventing a system designed to induce cooperation among the various players and thereby run itself (as I will be explaining), all Satoshi needed to do was introduce his ideas. Once the system was up and running, there was nothing anyone could do to stop it. Bitcoin now had a life of its own.

The groundbreaking innovation behind Satoshi's technology was the invention of software that creates a constantly updating ledger, the history of which cannot be changed. Until the invention of Bitcoin, the problem with digital records, including those used to manage the money we currently hold in the bank on a digital ledger, is that it can easily be changed. Up until now digital ledgers required a trusted intermediary to ensure the integrity of the records. In our financial system, historically, this has been the role of the central banks.

The way that Bitcoin has been designed means this intermediary is no longer required, or at least the intermediary is no longer human. The integrity of the Bitcoin system is based on math, on a software protocol.

Clearly this is an innovation that can have many uses, which is where the current "blockchain" craze has arisen from. With the whole of society now being undermined by the corruption in our existing financial system, however, the most critical benefit, specifically of the Bitcoin blockchain, is the use of the technology as a form of money, an irreversible ledger that can allow for ownership, exchange, and protection of an individual's digital property.

The Bitcoin software operates on a computer that is networked, or shared, with other computers. The software on each computer keeps in a file the list of all the transactions that have ever been completed on the network. By communicating with the other computer nodes the software continually updates this shared file with all the other computers whenever a new transaction is made. Thereby these interacting computers are said to operate by consensus. Each of the computers keeping track of all of the transactions on the Bitcoin blockchain is known as a "full node." It is these nodes that create the network and keep Bitcoin operating in a decentralized way. The more nodes there are, the stronger the network becomes.

New transactions are processed in blocks, creating a chain of connecting blocks and, as a result, this file is known as a blockchain. Adding new blocks to the blockchain, in order to validate transactions and ensure that each transaction is unique, is the challenging part of maintaining the blockchain. This is where mining comes in. Similar to gold, mining bitcoin involves the search for something very rare, in this case rare numbers. This rare number is known as a "proof-of-work."

Miners around the world search independently in a competition to find a proof-of-work that meets the criteria required by the Bitcoin network. It is then the job of the Bitcoin miners to process the most recent transactions from the updating nodes into a new block, by then validating this block of new transactions with a proof-of-work. As a result, they are then able to add the new block to the previously validated blocks already on the blockchain. The proof-of-work allows the new block to be accepted as validated by the nodes, updating the chain and allowing them to start accepting new transactions to be processed in the next block. If the miners try to sneak in a new block of transactions that don't meet the validation requirements, the nodes will reject that block.

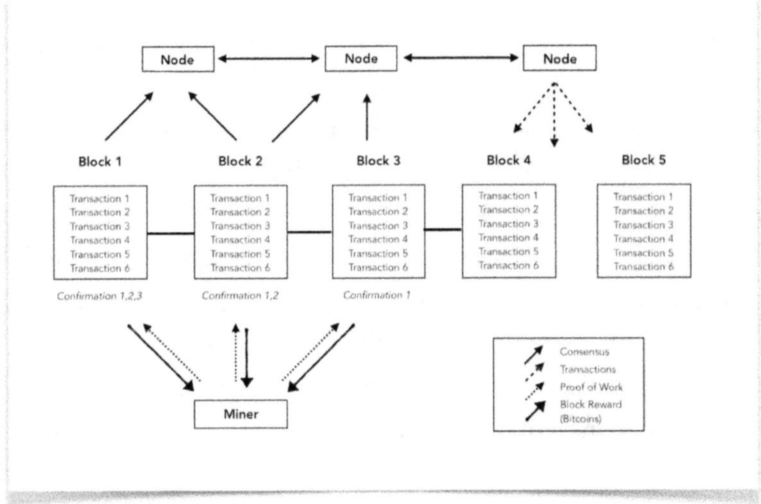

Construction of the Blockchain

Typically new blocks are being mined by finding the proof-of-work, and thus validating blocks and adding them to the blockchain every ten minutes. Once a transaction has been processed into a block, those attempting the transaction are able to see that the transaction has received a "confirmation," meaning that their transaction is now inside a validated block and is unlikely to be changed. The more confirmations a transaction has received, the more blocks have been added to the blockchain above the block holding the original transaction and, therefore, the more confident you can be that the transaction cannot be double-spent; that is, the same satoshis (a "satoshi" is a smaller denomination equal to one hundred millionth of a bitcoin) have not been used to make a simultaneous transaction elsewhere.

Before moving on I will quickly address the double-spend problem. It is possible to send two conflicting transactions into the network, such as an attempt to spend the same satoshis. The Bitcoin software solves this problem by forcing nodes to keep all the transactions they receive in a "memory" before writing them to a block.

At ten-minute intervals a random node on the network will add the transactions from their memory on to a block. This updated block is then shared with the network and validated by a miner. If validated, the nodes will accept the transactions in the updated block as "'correct," removing any conflicting transactions from their memory. As a result no double-spend transactions will ever be written to the blockchain and all nodes can update their files in agreement with one another.

Discovering these rare proof-of-work numbers and maintaining the blockchain requires power in the form of electricity. The interested parties on the network that supply this are the miners. In the early days it used to be possible to discover the rare proof-of-work numbers and mine bitcoin on a laptop computer, but as the network has grown, more power is required to compete and find these rare numbers in order to add a block to the blockchain. As an incentive to use power to process these transactions, miners collect a fee, paid by the person initiating the transaction: a small amount of satoshis for each Bitcoin transaction that is made.

In addition to the transaction fees, each new block that is added to the blockchain makes available to the miners a fixed amount of bitcoins that did not previously exist. Therefore if you are able to process or mine a block successfully, the Bitcoin software issues new bitcoins as a reward for your effort. This reward is known as a "block reward" and in 2019 currently stands at 12.5 bitcoin. Sometime in May 2020 this reward will be reduced to 6.25 bitcoin. This is because of an event known as "the halving," when the bitcoin reward "halves" after every 210,000 blocks have been validated and added to the blockchain.

Thus mining bitcoin becomes harder and harder as the network grows and each bitcoin becomes more expensive to create. It is estimated that the last bitcoin will be mined in 2140. At this point the miners will be reimbursed only with the transaction fees they receive for processing transactions.

The total reward that will ever be received from the Bitcoin network has been limited by the software that Satoshi designed to 21 million bitcoins. This is why Bitcoin is said to be digital gold.

Gold is valuable because you can't create more of it without some difficulty.

A monetary system based on gold is said to be "sound" because the value of the means of exchange is kept stable and can't easily be changed. By limiting the number of bitcoins that will ever be created, Satoshi created a digital system designed with the most useful economic properties of gold, as a form of sound money, in mind.

Contrary to fiat currencies that are now endlessly increasing their supply of dollars, pounds, and euros like a magic porridge pot, through debt creation by central banks, the total number of bitcoins created by the Bitcoin software will only ever be 21 million. Due to their digital nature these bitcoins are almost infinitely divisible. The total number of satoshis, designed as a unit of bitcoin, is 2.1 quadrillion. Ample enough at this point in time to absorb the purchasing power of the entire world.

The only thing influencing the value of what you can purchase for bitcoin or satoshis is the number of people using it in the network. As the network grows, the purchasing power of bitcoin grows. Those that understand this are taking the risk and investing in owning it now, because they realize the power of this new technology and the ability it gives individuals to preserve and grow their purchasing power in the future. This of course is predicated on Bitcoin fulfilling its destiny as a new world reserve currency, no longer requiring the control of central banks.

Blocks in the blockchain can be considered an individual safe where your coins are held as the last recognized transaction. In order to make a new transaction you need to select what you want to withdraw, "unlock" the block, and then lock it again once the amount withdrawn has been recorded on the ledger. This amount is then deposited in a new block that only the receiver can unlock when *they* wish to make a withdrawal.

To facilitate this process two types of "keys" are used: a public key and a private key. "Public-key cryptography" is the technology behind these keys, which operate by generating a random number. The public key is generated from your private key while keeping the private key a secret. A public key is one everyone can see, and this is typically displayed as a QR code, allowing you to receive a Bitcoin transaction. The private key is what allows you to unlock a transaction and transmit the digital value you are currently holding to someone else. Only you should have possession of the private key. Anyone else that has access to your private key is able to have free use of any bitcoins that you may be holding that are associated with that private key.

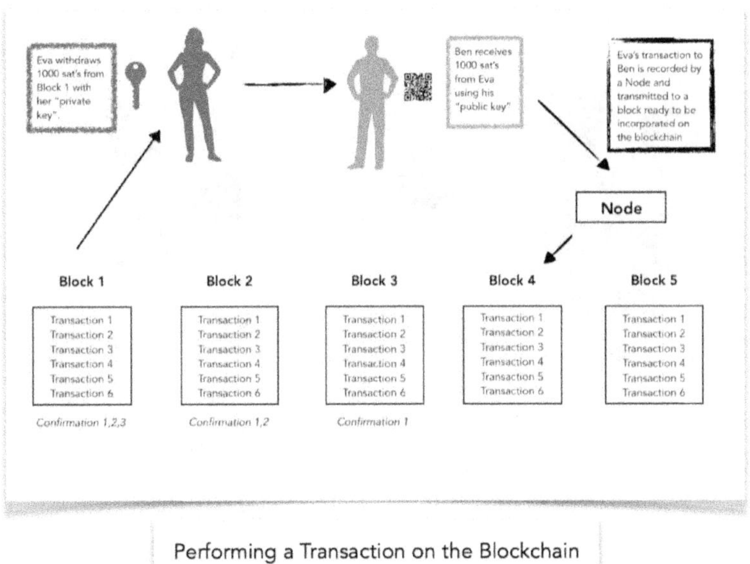

Performing a Transaction on the Blockchain

Your personal record of the bitcoins or satoshis you hold are stored in a "wallet." Bitcoin wallets are generally split into two categories: "hot" wallets and "cold" wallets. Hot wallets tend to be held on a mobile device, such as your phone, using a Bitcoin wallet app. There are many types of these. "Cold" wallets are also known as "hardware" wallets—these are designed to store your bitcoin funds on a hardware device that does not connect to the internet in order to keep your funds held more securely. I will be going into these in more detail later in the book. For now what you need to know is that each type of wallet will generate your private key, normally as a list of twelve to twenty-four English words that you then record somewhere safe and confidential. This string of words will enable you to re-create your wallet anywhere in the world, hot or cold, as long as your have access to those words, even if they are only in your memory—clever, huh!

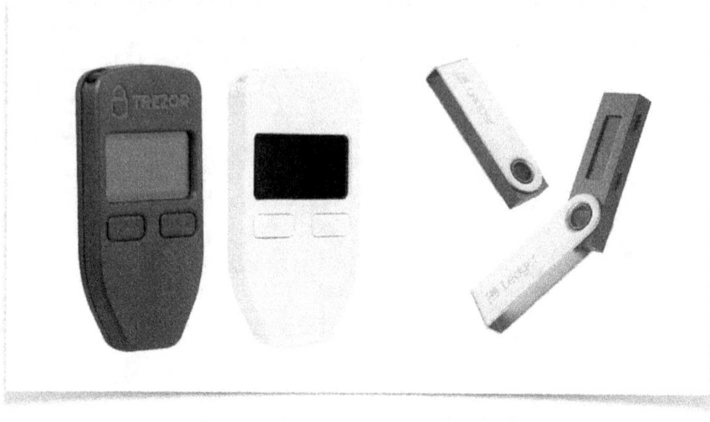

Examples of Hardware Wallets

This is what makes Bitcoin potentially so dangerous to the world's existing financial system, but so incredibly useful for the world's population. Not only does the design of the software enable you to preserve value in an asset that cannot be stolen from you (unless you are careless with your private key), but it can be transported anywhere in the world without any authority knowing about it, until it is spent. Imagine being a refugee who has to leave all of their worldly belongings behind—as long as you can remember the private key to your Bitcoin wallet you can at least take some of your assets with you to a new place. There you will have something of value with which you are able to start again.

The Bitcoin software code is "open-source," which means the code can be seen by everyone, and anyone in the world is able to suggest changes to the code. Changes to the code can be proposed by any developer, but new changes will only be approved by agreement with all the nodes, once the new code has been fully discussed, agreed upon, and approved. The agreement is finalized when each node incorporates the new updated software onto their computers. If the nodes disagree with the proposed changes then they won't update their software.

This is what happened when the software upgrade to Segwit was adopted in 2017. There were those in the Bitcoin community who felt strongly that the Segwit upgrade should not be adopted, so a "hard fork" was created. This is where all of the previous transactions on the Bitcoin blockchain were copied, and new transactions continued to be processed, without using the new software upgrade. The hard fork that still operates on the original Bitcoin source code but without the Segwit upgrade is now known as "Bitcoin Cash."

Segwit was an upgrade designed to improve the scalability features of Bitcoin. The Bitcoin developers promoting Segwit were keen to keep the block sizes small, as this facilitates smaller computers operating as nodes to help Bitcoin keep its decentralized features. To do this they wanted to introduce new features to allow smaller transactions to take place off the main chain, using protocols such as "Lightning," which enables smaller transactions to be processed faster and requires smaller fees.

The promoters of Bitcoin Cash, in contrast, wanted to make the block sizes bigger in order to process more transactions and increase the scalability of the network, but the supporters of Segwit argued that this meant that eventually the block sizes would get so big it would be difficult to process the transactions without much bigger computers, thereby making Bitcoin by default more centralized. The result for the holders of bitcoin, following the hard fork, was that anyone holding bitcoin prior to August 2017 received an equivalent amount of bitcoin cash in addition to the bitcoin they were already holding.

Both the Bitcoin and Bitcoin Cash blockchains had the freedom to proceed with what they felt was right, but eventually the majority of the market voted for the Segwit adoption by selling the bitcoin cash they had received, created by the hard fork, for the bitcoin that adopted Segwit. As a result of more people doing this and continuing to believe in the Segwit upgrade, as of 2019 Bitcoin has a higher value in the market than Bitcoin Cash.

In this way cryptocurrencies are very democratic. The users have as much of an influence on how the Bitcoin software progresses as the developers do. If they feel that the development of Bitcoin is ultimately losing its way, they have an opportunity to "vote" by choosing to switch to the software that they feel is right. This will be an added disincentive to the developers to introduce an upgrade that is unpopular and, even more important, a reason for people to stay informed as to what is happening at a protocol level.

Clearly as Bitcoin becomes more and more established, switching to another protocol will be harder and harder to do, but these philosophical battles in Bitcoin's early stages help to demonstrate how the software has developed and led to the Bitcoin that we now have today.

As a result of these mechanisms, a consensus is required in order to change anything in the software protocol. This consensus helps to keep the network stable and secure. The decentralized nature of the network and the unanimity required to change the protocol means that no individual can pass a law to change how the software works.

The rules of how Bitcoin works are programmed into the software. As an investor you vote for those rules by buying bitcoin and using it as a form of money, or you don't. This is why even though there are now numerous other cryptocurrencies, Bitcoin is currently the most valuable. Those that understand are voting with their government currencies for the protocol that they believe is the strongest. At this moment in time that is seen as Bitcoin. It might have been the first cryptocurrency to establish itself, but most investors and users still believe it is the best, which is why Bitcoin is the cryptocurrency that currently costs the most to acquire.

The features of Bitcoin, as described here, are what make it extremely valuable. As a result it is increasingly being seen as the best form of money that has ever been known.

No single entity has control over Bitcoin. It has now been around for over ten years, and in that time has spread to almost every corner of the world. Mocked and ridiculed initially, after ten years there is no denying the increasing numbers of people around the world who are coming to see just how valuable this new technology is. It is an opportunity to preserve the quality of their savings, as the quality of their existing money is rapidly degrading due to central banks around the world, facilitated by governments, printing debt faster than the eye can see.

These centralized organizations have now dug themselves such a hole, due to their bad financial management, that it will soon become apparent to their populations that if they want the ability to take control of their lives, they need to control their own assets and start exchanging their goods and services for something that will preserve its value. At the moment it may seem as though Bitcoin has a price that fluctuates wildly, but that is because the total value of the network is still relatively small and the market is mainly full of speculators buying low and selling high.

Small businesses are the lifeblood of any economy. These businesses are currently being crushed, like sheep to the slaughter, by the corruption of the existing financial system—a system that we have all been forced to operate within due to the absence of a better choice.

Bitcoin is our opportunity to make a new choice now and try to correct the errors of the past.

Are You Ready to Change?

NOVEMBER 2007—I WAS reading my solicitor the riot act. It had already taken over a year to sort out the lease agreement with the hairdressers for my little business, and I was seven months pregnant. Now the landlord who owned the building where the hairdressers operated had decided that he wanted to practically rewrite the whole thing! On top of this, the hairdressers, who were going to be my landlords, were arguing with me as to whether VAT was included in the rent they had already quoted me eighteen months before. I was ready to tear my hair out. There were many signs that maybe pushing ahead was a bad idea, obstacles in my path from the universe constantly telling me, "Don't go this way!" But I was stubborn, and in all honesty I didn't know what else to do.

I was tired and frustrated working for others. My favorite job up until this point had been working as a dentist as part of a chain of clinics operated by Boots the Chemist in the UK. I lived close to their head office and I worked two days a week there and three days a week in two of their dental clinics. I loved this combination. I was working with a wider range of people as opposed to just being stuck in one room, working in people's mouths all day.

Unfortunately Boots closed their dental project in late 2004, and although I continued to work with the business that took over, it was not the same. It ended up as an exercise in watching everything I had previously loved die. Observing everyone else get it wrong (as I perceived it) was annoying to me. Working for myself was now my only option.

With the looming financial crisis, my timing was very bad, though I had no idea about this at the time. I had tunnel vision, focusing on my own goals—why should bigger issues going on out of my awareness affect me? I was destined to learn the hard way, and so I did.

Being a dentist is a challenging job. Keeping up with all the rules that are constantly being introduced or changed by the myriad bodies that have a stake in controlling dental care, even while working for someone else, is exhausting. Trying to set up a business is more challenging still. As I graduated with a business degree in 2006, I should have been more aware of all this than most of my colleagues. In truth, I suppose all it really did was make me overconfident. Although I knew the theory about how to manage and market a business, and how to understand contracts and limited companies, putting this knowledge into practice is a very different thing. My education on the wider world still required more depth, as I was about to discover.

The 2008 financial crisis was an unexpected shock to my financial planning and how I expected to be living my life in my early thirties. What would have been tricky but possible (even with a new baby) only two years previously, now became a living nightmare. Fortunately my ego wasn't too closely attached to my financial resources, even if my circumstances were less comfortable. Ultimately my motivation had been to create something that was professionally satisfying, not only for myself but for the results I could then deliver to my patients and the working environment I could create for my staff. It was this sense of adventure that kept me going, and it meant that I was able to emerge successfully, by selling the business profitably ten years later—but trust me, it was a difficult journey.

I sometimes wonder how many others are in a similar situation right now. The damage from the financial crisis in 2008 was mitigated through quantitative easing. Which essentially meant providing more liquidity (debt) into the financial system, to prevent all of the assets that currently rely on that debt from collapsing in value. But world debt has been growing even faster since then—nothing has been fixed. The UK government has been bleating about austerity for the past ten years, but as we approach another set of elections in December 2019, everyone's pledge is about spending and ending austerity. Not because anything is fixed, mind you, but because now no one can afford to care.

"With Brexit on the horizon, disaster is looming anyway, so let's throw all caution to the wind and continue spending. It will at least get us elected, so we have a chance to sort things out our way!"

Oh, it is so over—these people are done!

When control structures collapse, how does life carry on? It is done by those on the ground who are managing their everyday lives, caring for others, and keeping things going as best they can. Throughout the centuries being able to exchange value is how human beings learned to interact fairly with each other. In the most prosperous periods of history, such as the Greek and Roman Empires and even the British Empire, this interaction was facilitated by gold. The phrase "'sound as a pound" comes from the time when the British had the reserve currency of the world, and the value of one ounce of gold was set at a standard of £4. This consistent value of the currency ensured that business deals were fair and equitable.

By the time Richard Nixon took the dollar off the gold standard in 1971, the price of gold was at £17 per ounce, and as of November 2019 it stands at £1,150 per ounce. Anyone who tells you our currency is not losing value is lying to you!

The only way for us to reintroduce fairness into our society is to start using sound money again. Clearly as a business owner I do not want the inconvenience of only accepting gold and silver coins. Paper notes were introduced into the monetary system long ago to overcome the inconvenience of this.

The problem with paper notes, as with all fiat currencies, is that a trusted third party is needed to ensure that the paper holds its value.

Fractional reserve banking, where banks are allowed to lend out multiples of what they hold in reserve; quantitative easing, where central banks make unlimited purchases of government securities; and modern monetary theory and Keynesian economics in general have now destroyed this trust.

Eventually all fiat currencies collapse. History has shown this time and time again. The fiat currencies that now proliferate around the world have lasted longer than almost any others in history. When currencies collapse, such episodes tend to be disastrous for the general population.

As a solution they start to save in the best currency available that will preserve its value. Last time this happened, in eastern Europe, that currency was the dollar. What if this time the dollar is the problem? Where will they go? At the moment the central banks of Russia and China are busy building their gold reserves, but will gold be where people run to the next time? I think not. Gold is too inconvenient now as a medium of exchange, and recent history has shown that governments and central banks cannot be trusted to maintain their currencies as a value against gold.

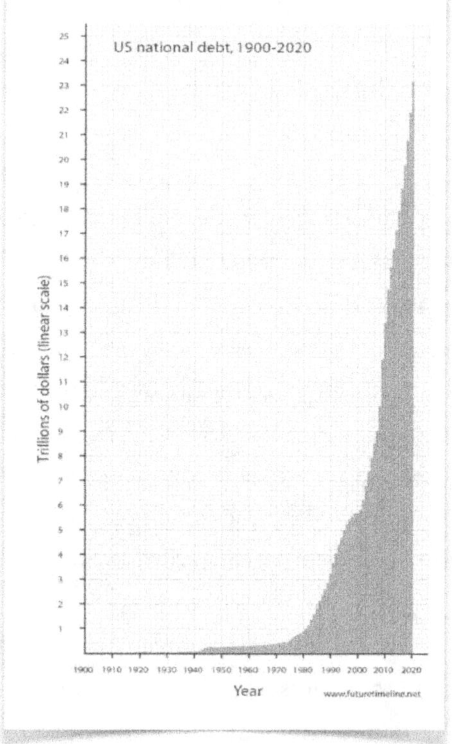

Out of Control Debt Since the
USA Came off the Gold Standard in 1971

Bitcoin, which has been deliberately programmed to replicate the economic qualities of gold while reducing the features which make it a hindrance, fixes this. Its software features—the QR code, public key, blockchain—instantly reduce fraud. Transactions are automatically entered on a digital ledger, enabling a business or an individual effectively to track payments while ensuring that no one can inflate its value.

There may well be some issues with having all of our transactions on a single database, as is the case with Bitcoin. This is a subject I will address later, but having our transactions entered in a database that is designed to preserve value fairly, compatible with the digital modern world, is to me the next logical step. Those that don't currently understand this will very quickly understand it once the next crisis hits.

As currencies start to lose their value, prices start to edge up and the quality of products starts to lower. History suggests that while this process builds slowly at first, once a tipping point is reached this trajectory increases faster and faster until one day, in the blink of an eye, a loaf of bread no longer costs £1, but £10. Before you know it wheelbarrows of paper currency are required to pay for something that was only pennies a few years before. This can destroy a business, as the ability to handle their finances competently, pay their bills, and reward their staff becomes increasingly impossible.

In this situation, however, if you have already put in place the processes and taken the time to understand the technology in order to accept Bitcoin as an alternative payment method, your chances of survival are going to be much higher. This is because as fiat money will be increasingly losing its value, Bitcoin will be increasingly preserving its value. So as fiat currency buys less and less, the bitcoin you own will be able to purchase more and more. We are already seeing this, although most are unaware of it. With one bitcoin you can in 2019 buy ten times as much as you could just three years ago. This will continue as the network becomes more robust and more people are incentivized to join the system.

At the moment, not many understand this, so Bitcoin tends to be ridiculed or seen as the money of drug dealers or funny internet money, but one day it could save your business, your family's finances, and/or even your life. Those that understand this are the ones that are buying it now. The sensible businesses are the ones that are learning about it now and choosing to inform their clients and customers about it.

Now, in 2019, I am wiser. I can see the next financial crisis brewing on the horizon, but how many other business owners—juggling staff, property, finances, and regulations while trying to remain profitable—can say the same? Once I understood what was happening, I sold my business while I still could and took some time out to study the problems further and figure out where the solutions may be—not just for me, but for all those others out there who cannot afford to take the time out to try to understand this, no matter how clever they may be.

My philosophy, once I understood the dangers in the financial system, was that if I were going to continue to operate my business in an environment where hyperinflation was creating chaos for everyone, I would need my customers to be financially stable. If all of my clients suddenly found themselves in financial dire straits, my business would die overnight. By introducing them to Bitcoin, however, I could encourage them to learn about this asset. So when the time of crisis arrives, they would already know about a place where they could store their savings. Meaning they would still have a means of paying if they need my services—everyone hates a toothache, after all. That is even worse than having no money!

Now that you know a bit more about the financial system and the history of money, and a lot more about Bitcoin, I want to close section one by asking you a few questions.

Are your finances, either as an individual or business, prepared for an impending crisis?

Is learning about Bitcoin and starting to accept it as a payment, either as an individual or in your business, something you would now consider?

Are you ready to change?

How?
The Present

CHAPTER FIVE

Acquisition

IN JULY 2016 I had just returned from attending a cruise in Alaska with Abraham Hicks Publications. The UK vote for Brexit was in and the price of gold and silver had just achieved an upwards pop in price. This was interesting. I had reached a stage with my business where things had improved greatly and it was operating in a stable fashion. It was time to think about what was next. My original plan had been to start my business with a little room in the hairdressing salon then move it to a new location which would allow my business to grow in a bigger environment. By this time I was now working with a business coach and we were thinking about what would be needed to fulfill this ambition.

The first task my coach gave me was to draw up a business plan with a cash flow forecast. The result of this task was depressing. I remember the excitement I felt when I drew up my original business plan for my current little business—at the time it felt like the world was full of wondrous possibilities. Now that I knew more about how the financial system worked and saw the signs of chaos on the horizon, I felt less enthused. The risks felt too big now. The issues and legislation in the business of dentistry were becoming suffocating. I had to admit that after experiencing the previous ten years, this was not how I wanted the next ten years to be. I didn't want to continue on with what I had started. I didn't mind climbing a ladder towards success, but this ladder felt as though it was against the wrong wall.

Nevertheless, I didn't know what I would prefer to do instead. By this stage I had become fascinated by the problems in the financial system. It had helped me to understand so much about why the NHS operated in the way that it did, and why so much in society appeared to be problematic. Understanding the problem was one thing though; where were the solutions? So my business carried on and I continued to ponder. It was during this summer that I decided to look at Bitcoin properly. I had heard about it, but only through the occasional mention and on the news. It had caught my attention but not enough for me to research it. Now was the time for me to address that.

So I started a Google search. There was information available through some websites and via YouTube, but a lot of it was very incohesive. Watching some of the videos and exploring some of the websites was like jumping into a story right in the middle. There was no one telling you the beginning, the middle, or the end. You had to catch a thread and follow it back to the beginning. Along the way you might pick up pieces of the puzzle that you could come back and look at later. Once put together, these pieces hopefully gave you a better understanding of the story.

Eventually I figured out that it was possible to purchase bitcoins via a very easy-to-use website called Coinbase, and so my first purchase occurred there. I set up an account, made a purchase using my debit card, and "voila": I owned some bitcoin! There they were, some new digits in my app, under the category "Bitcoin." This was very exciting. The most fun thing about it though, was watching the price go up.

I was very lucky; my interest had been piqued just following the 2016 halving (a halving is when the block reward for miners is halved, as explained in chapter three). The Bitcoin miners were now instantly receiving half the reward they had before when mining a block, creating an immediate shortage of supply.

The 2016 halving was only the second one since Bitcoin's inception. On analyzing a price chart of Bitcoin after the first halving in November 2012, the price appears to follow a particular trajectory. Immediately following the halving the price has an initial drop, as the miners sell bitcoin previously mined to pay their bills.

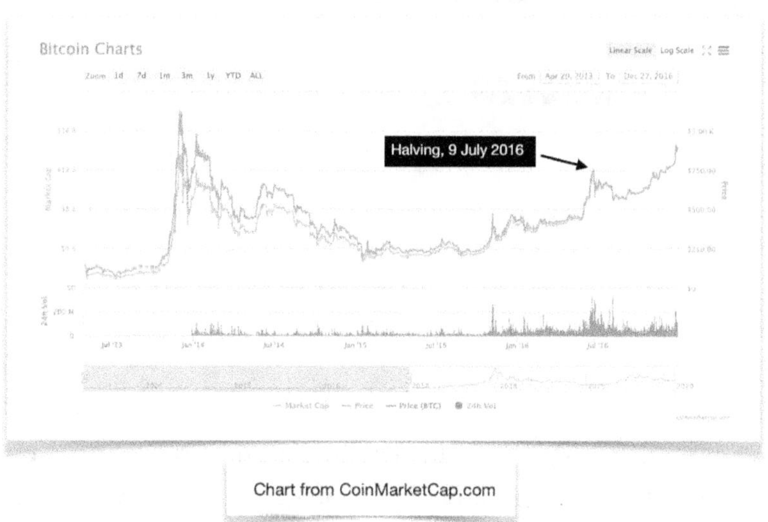

Chart from CoinMarketCap.com

Following this initial drop the price starts to creep up, as there are fewer bitcoins coming onto the market, to be sold, from the miners. As it does this, speculators become interested, creating a positive feedback loop over the following twelve to eighteen months. The price then escalates to a frenzied peak, only to be sharply followed by a crash as the speculators cash in their gains before the price settles again, usually somewhere above the previous parabolic peak. New investors usually enter the market during this time. Their curiosity piqued, these new investors often research the new technology prior to investing in it. Once they understand it, rather than speculating they are now not prepared to risk selling it, no matter how much the price drops! This provides a supportive floor under the price.

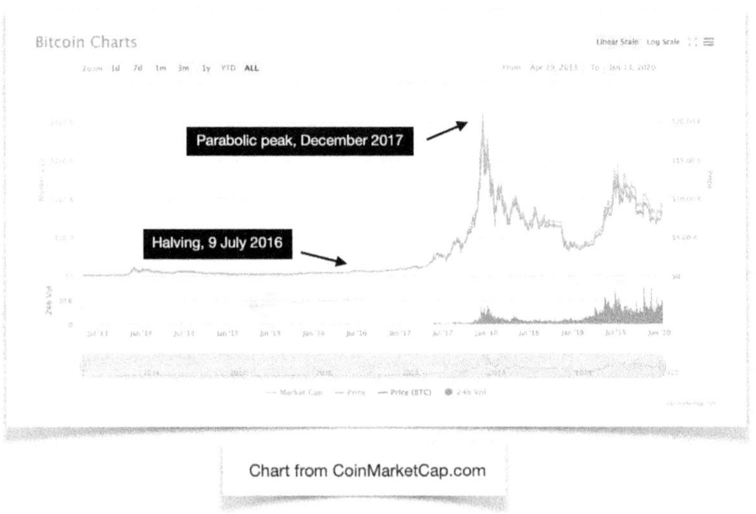

Chart from CoinMarketCap.com

Finally, six months prior to the next halving the price starts to creep up again as the miners attempt to build up their savings pot in anticipation of the next halving, before the cycle begins all over again.

This is a casual observation of the way in which the price of Bitcoin currently seems to move and it appears to be a dynamic directly related to how bitcoins are created through mining.

These fundamental dynamics of how bitcoins are created is programmed into the software, so it is unlikely to change unless there is a consensus agreement to alter the software. This would suggest that this flow of the price will be likely to continue in a similar fashion if left to its own devices. Now, unfortunately, the traditional financial marketplace has exchange-traded funds (ETFs) set up for Bitcoin trading, which may have some influence in managing the price. I will explore the implications of this later in the book in further detail.

I was not aware of this price dynamic in 2016; I was just a complete (albeit very lucky) newbie finding my way. Almost every day when I opened that app for the next eighteen months the value of my little bitcoin holding was gradually creeping up. It was an intoxicating thing to watch. As my understanding grew of the potential of this technology, I began more and more to appreciate its value. I became infatuated with learning as much as I could, whenever I could spare the time.

As I studied and watched, I came across reports about Bitcoin's history and a significant event that occurred in February of 2014. At this time 70 percent of the world's bitcoin was being bought and sold through a Bitcoin exchange based in Tokyo called Mount Gox.

Although Bitcoin as a digital asset operates in a decentralized way, if you want to buy and sell it between fiat currencies and other digital coins or tokens, you normally make these transactions on an exchange. This means the bitcoin you own has to be sent to an exchange and is often held there while the trading of these coins and tokens takes place. Once on the exchange, the private keys to these bitcoins are then controlled by the exchange.

The Bitcoin exchanges in 2019 work in a similar fashion to a bank, in that they only keep a percentage of their assets in reserve. As long as they have, say, 10 percent in reserve, and as long as enough people trust that organization so that they are not all claiming their assets at the same time, the bank or exchange can continue to operate with "manufactured digits" that do not equate to the true amount of assets that they hold. For example, they may hold one thousand bitcoins, but then allow trading of ten thousand bitcoins on their books. If you think this is shocking, take a moment to look up how fractional reserve banking works. Banks have been doing this with your money for the past one hundred years, and look how that has turned out.

So in 2014, the price of Bitcoin started to drop after hitting its recent parabolic peak of $1,300 in November 2013. As the peak in price passed, many of the speculators wanted to sell to preserve their gains. To make matters worse, rumors of a hack on the Mount Gox exchange led to even more investors wanting to sell. But, in Bitcoin exchanges as in traditional banking, if everyone wants to sell at once, this creates a problem. It turned out Mount Gox did not own the number of bitcoins it was meant to have. Result: Mount Gox prevented withdrawals and then went bankrupt, its assets were liquidated, and everyone who had their bitcoins stored on the exchange had them confiscated. The owners of these bitcoins are still waiting for the case to be resolved.

The golden rule for Bitcoiners following this event is *not* to store your coins on an exchange!

This was a hard lesson, but history tells us these problems are doomed to be repeated as time passes and people forget. Operating on exchanges is not ideal, but they are a necessary evil while a new system builds in parallel with the old. Once people are making payments to each other using Bitcoin and we have a new financial system with Bitcoin as the base layer, bitcoins will be circulating widely in society, and centralized exchanges won't be needed as much anymore.

That said, there are decentralized exchanges, like Veritaseum, that are designed to keep track of digital assets without needing a centralized entity. These will be more prevalent in the future. Some time and development is needed, though, before we are there. In the meantime, those who possess bitcoin remember their golden rule with a simple saying: "Not your keys, not your coins," meaning that while your bitcoin is stored on an exchange, that exchange owns the private key to your bitcoin and in reality may only truly control a small percentage of the bitcoin they maintain that you own.

To rectify this situation you need to withdraw your coins from an exchange and store them on a wallet where you control the private key. As explained in chapter three, there are two categories you can choose from here: a hot wallet stored on your phone, which is risky and has the potential to be hacked, so it is normally recommended that you only store a small amount of satoshis here for everyday transactions; or a cold wallet, which is a device that is not connected to the internet. Some people create paper wallets by storing their private key on a piece of paper that they file away securely. An easier solution is to use a hardware wallet, such as a Trezor or a Ledger Nano.

Paper wallets are difficult to generate safely because you need to use equipment where everything is offline. This is to ensure that a potential hacker of your computer cannot see your private key while you generate it. I personally have never tried this method. Hardware wallets are much easier to use. If you buy one (always directly from the manufacturer) they come with instructions that are simple to follow.

The first thing the hardware wallet will do when you plug it in to your computer is generate the seed words associated with your private key. These are the twelve to twenty-four English words I mentioned in chapter three. The device shows them to you on a screen that is protected, by being separated from the screen on your computer, helping you to keep them secure.

Once you have recorded your private key and stored it safely (*not* online), you can then arrange to withdraw the bitcoin you have purchased on an exchange on to your own hardware wallet. The hardware wallet will generate public addresses (QR codes) associated with your private key. You then use one of these addresses to receive the bitcoin that has been sent to you from an exchange. Once received, this bitcoin can only then be sent to someone else by being unlocked by the private key on your hardware wallet.

Once the private keys to your bitcoin are fully in your control, no one else can take them away from you, unless they have access to your private key.

"Not your keys, not your coins."

In essence, if cryptocurrency exchanges are equivalent to banks, hardware wallets are equivalent to a locked safe in your home. You do not need to rely on a third party or an intermediary to protect your assets. They are also easier to protect because they are small and more easily hidden. You could even destroy the hardware wallet if there was a threat of it being discovered and stolen. You would still be able to recover your funds as long as you can remember the seed words that generate your private key and have access to a computer connected to the internet.

Before I transferred my bitcoin to a hardware wallet, I had some fun using my Coinbase account. I asked almost everyone I knew (who were prepared to listen) to download the Coinbase app. I would then transfer a million satoshis to them, equivalent to about £10 at the time. (As a reminder, one bitcoin is equivalent to one hundred million satoshis.) Then I'd enthusiastically demonstrate to them how this new technology worked.

I also experimented with the website Purse.io which allows you to purchase goods on Amazon at a discount if you pay in bitcoin. The process was fiddly and time-consuming. The wait for the goods was typically longer than through the normal transaction method. I had a great time though, figuring out how it worked, and was able to buy a cute little heater for my home with the profits I made from the price rises at the end of 2016. I effectively purchased it for free—I was stoked!

These experiments solidified my understanding and helped me see the huge potential for this technology. If I could purchase goods from Amazon, why couldn't my clients purchase my services using bitcoin? I didn't see why not, and I also saw the potential for offering my clients an alternative to the persistently broken card machine that would regularly make me break out in a cold sweat. I could also avoid any shenanigans next time the online banking system unexpectedly delayed depositing the payments from my clients into my bank account (after they had deducted their appropriate fee, of course).

Not only this, but I could protect my savings from being confiscated by the bank.

"Bail-in" laws had been quietly solidified in the EU by 2016. The new legislation required each member country to confer on bank regulators the power to write down, modify the terms of, cancel completely, and/or convert into equity the liabilities of a failing bank before it becomes insolvent.

The conditions for this had been tested in 2013 when depositors in two Cypriot banks lost billions when savings were confiscated to protect the island's banking system (this process is now known as a "bail-in"). The move was a condition sought by international creditors for a €10 billion ($11.62 billion) bailout to the east Mediterranean island.

Who knows when a similar circumstance could play out in the UK, US, or any other country for that matter? Businesses are normally more likely to have significant savings in a bank than individuals. A confiscation on this scale could have dire consequences on the viability of a business. It is good to have another option now that bank confiscation is a distinct possibility and has been definitively established in law and practice.

In addition to protecting my savings, I could also collect an asset as payment from my clients that was likely to increase in value, rather than decrease, as was clearly happening with my fiat savings in the bank.

One of the issues I often experienced as a private dentist, in comparison to being an NHS dentist, is that I would often receive comments about the prices of my services being so much higher than receiving an equivalent service on the NHS. There were good reasons for this, but it saddened me that this was often a barrier to some people's ability to access what I could offer. So it occurred to me that if I could help them feel wealthier, maybe they wouldn't have such a strong objection to paying my fees, particularly if I had helped them achieve this.

My mind was made up—it was time to introduce my newfound knowledge into my own business and see what effect this would have.

CHAPTER SIX

Money in Motion

AFTER ATTENDING SOME Bitcoin meetups at the end of 2016, I was starting to make some knowledgeable friends in the Bitcoin community. So I reached out to them to ask whether they knew of the best way for a business to accept bitcoin. The main answer that came back was to use a payment intermediary; a company called BitPay was the place to go at the time. This company would allow you to accept bitcoin as a payment and would then immediately convert it back to your local currency. I wasn't keen on this—it seemed to defeat the object of what Bitcoin, as a new form of currency, was about. The last thing I wanted was another intermediary to deal with; my card machine was giving me enough headaches as it was!

Eventually I discovered the Blockchain Merchant app, specifically designed for small businesses to accept bitcoin. I still had an old iPhone 5S in storage, so I recovered and recharged it and downloaded Blockchain Merchant. This allowed me to set up a merchant account very easily. This neat little app calculated the correct portion of bitcoin, based on what I was charging the client, then generated a QR code that the client could scan to settle the bill. Easy peasy. Not only this, the bitcoin received went immediately into a Bitcoin wallet, the private keys over which I had complete control.

Once I had established the way in which I would accept payment, the next step was to introduce it to my clients. I displayed the Bitcoin logo along with some business leaflets at the front desk, just in front of the computer. I also had an instruction notice on the main window outside, so that even pedestrians that walked past could read it if they so desired. The information leaflet was included with every patient treatment plan, and I notified them on my website that I was now accepting bitcoin as a payment method. I was good to go.

Leaflet at the Front Door and Desk Signage, January 2017

So setting up the ability to pay in bitcoin was extremely easy. An additional part of the task was training the staff. This consisted mainly of showing them how to use the app on the iPhone. I then created a new category of payment on the practice software system that allowed us to identify when someone had paid in bitcoin. After a brief session to show them how to use the new app, I also demonstrated to them how it worked by asking them to download the Coinbase app onto their own smartphones, and then transferring to each of them £10 in bitcoin. All that was left was for the first client to come in and offer to pay using this new payment method.

Everything was set up by mid-January 2017—then nothing, nothing, nothing. I finally received one offer by a client to pay in bitcoin in December 2017!

This wasn't due to lack of interest. In my enthusiasm, I was telling everyone about it. Many were happy to engage with me on the subject, while others frowned uncertainly, having only heard about Bitcoin in the news associated with various unmentionables, like fraudsters, criminals, and drug dealers.

However, the price rise of Bitcoin that year was unbelievable. I suspect that many of my clients who were interested looked into owning some. Once they did, they may well have preferred to hold on to it and see what it would do, rather than spend it on dentistry services. This behavior is reflected in a monetary principle known as Gresham's Law which states that "bad money drives out good." This means that money that is losing value rapidly will drive out of circulation money that is more stable in value. This is because most people will want to dispose of (i.e., spend) the money that is losing value before accessing the more-stable money that they have saved. Nobody wants to dip into their nest egg, designed to last long term, unless they have to. This is the rainy day money.

So the reality is, at this moment in time, while everything is relatively stable, most people who understand the value of Bitcoin are not likely to part with it for your goods and services unless they have an incentive to do so. This wasn't entirely surprising to me as I understood what I was doing. I didn't offer the opportunity to pay in bitcoin to my clients because I thought it would generate an influx of new customers desperate to spend their bitcoins. I did it because I wanted to make my clients aware of a new payment method, giving them the opportunity to learn about Bitcoin before they really needed it. I believe I achieved this objective with some of them.

Gresham's Law, in addition, states that in a hyperinflationary crisis the principle of "bad money driving out good money" is reversed. This is because the bad money is by then losing value so quickly that it effectively becomes useless. So the only way for commerce to continue adequately is for people to start exchanging the better money. This is what I believe we ought to be preparing for.

If the rate at which prices increase starts to speed up, due to the ongoing devaluation of the fiat currencies around the world, businesses and individuals will be better able to protect themselves by accepting a means of payment that will hold its value.

In ancient times when hyperinflation occurred—the earliest recorded instance was in Egypt in 276 AD—populations eventually returned to gold. Even in recent history, in Weimar Germany, the population ended up having to store their savings in gold, if they were able to access it. Gold has held its quality as a form of sound money for over five thousand years. It has been a reliable store of wealth and traditionally an excellent means for human beings to exchange value with each other.

When hyperinflation occurs, the only possible solution is to seek out the most stable form of money available and start using that as a means of exchange. It is the only way to end the madness. Next time this happens, will we return to gold?

As explained previously, there are two good reasons I believe this is unlikely. Gold is inconvenient to hold and transact with. Even if the banks continue to operate by holding gold, no one is going to trust them now to monitor the value of the currency against the gold they are holding. They have had their opportunity to be the masters of money, and they have been found wanting, to the detriment of everyone. Their time is done.

As Bitcoin is a new technology, the system is developing at a rapid rate. When I was looking into accepting Bitcoin as a payment method in my business, BitPay was seen as the best way for businesses to accept bitcoin. This method, however, relied on converting the bitcoin immediately into the local fiat currency. The idea was that this would help to shield the business from wild fluctuations in Bitcoin's value. Indeed the price of Bitcoin has been known to increase by a factor of twenty in the space of months, as it did between January and December 2017, rising from a price of $900 to $20,000, only to lose more than 80 percent of its value from January to December 2018, going from a price of $17,700 to $3,200. In this situation accepting Bitcoin as a form of payment could give a business significant trouble when trying to manage its cash flow.

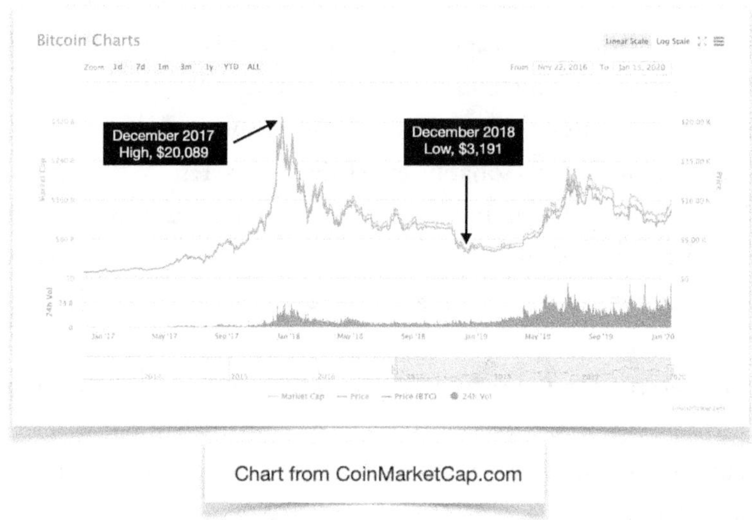

Chart from CoinMarketCap.com

Fortunately, as payments in bitcoin are still pretty rare, as explained above, the consequences of this are fairly negligible right now. In fact, many businesses that were persuaded to accept payment in bitcoin in the early days eventually dropped it due to lack of interest from their customers. The eager Bitcoiners wanting to spend their bitcoin were few and far between.

An additional problem is the scalability of the Bitcoin network. In order to ensure that a particular transaction has been added to the blockchain, there is usually a ten-minute delay before the transaction is transferred from the memory of the node onto the blockchain, as explained in chapter three. In order to ensure that the transaction has been added to the blockchain, the receiver is advised to wait to receive a confirmation, which is a notification from the system that the transaction has been accepted and processed into a block by one of the miners.

Generally, receiving three confirmations is seen as good practice. Until these confirmations are received the transaction is potentially invalid. Or the bitcoin/satoshis could be double-spent. When the network is busy, these transactions can take a long time and the transaction fees can become unreasonably expensive. As a result, due to these limitations, many maintain that Bitcoin cannot be used as a currency. It cannot handle a similar volume of transactions as Visa—one of the current big-name payment intermediaries.

This has been a long-standing debate in the development of Bitcoin. By 2017 philosophies on the subject had divided into two camps. Initially Satoshi set the block size limit to 1 MB, which meant that the amount of data in a block could continue to be handled by smaller nodes. One camp consisted of those who felt that allowing bigger blocks should be the answer to Bitcoin's scaling problem. Many others argued, however, that this would just delay the inevitable moment in the future when the size of blocks would need to be increased again. Also, by allowing blocks to get too big it would affect Bitcoin's ability to remain decentralized, as it would not be possible for the entire blockchain to be updated by the smaller nodes.

An alternative solution was to add new rules to the network via a software upgrade known as "Segregated Witness," or Segwit, as mentioned previously. This software upgrade implemented changes in how the transactions were handled in each of the blocks, meaning they could now handle larger numbers of payments. In addition it would allow the development of new technology systems, such as Lightning, a Layer 2 payment protocol that operates on top of the Bitcoin network.

Lightning is designed to enable fast transactions among participating nodes. Use of the Lightning Network normally consists of entering a payment transaction to Bitcoin on (Layer 1), followed by making a number of Lightning exchanges between the Lightning channels without broadcasting these back to the Bitcoin blockchain. Once these exchanges are complete the Lightning channel can then be closed by broadcasting the final version of the settlement payment back to the Bitcoin blockchain, to distribute the channel's funds. In this way smaller transactions can be more easily and cheaply processed via the creation of Lightning nodes and the use of Lightning channels.

The issues at the time caused much debate. In the end Segwit was adopted. Those that objected created an alternative chain of the network, known as a hard fork, copying all the previous transactions but then continuing to mine a separate chain of blocks without the addition of Segwit. This new chain is now known as Bitcoin Cash.

This meant that everyone who held bitcoin before mid-July 2017 now had an equivalent amount of bitcoin and bitcoin cash. Veterans of the space who had been arguing for Segwit's implementation for almost two years now breathed a sigh of relief and promptly sold their bitcoin cash for bitcoin. This was probably the largest contributor to the exponential price rise of Bitcoin at the end of 2017.

As the introduction of Segwit enables Lightning, this means that the possibilities for payments have now been thrown wide open. Custodial solutions such as BitPay, that still rely entirely on fiat currencies, are no longer the primary options. This is excellent news because if you, like me, want to accept Bitcoin as a payment method, the best practice for accepting it is to receive transactions directly into a wallet where you control the private keys.

Let's take a moment to get into some of the concrete details you'll need to know to accept bitcoin as an individual or business.

Each transaction on the Bitcoin network requires a fee by the sender. So ideally—especially when the transaction is large—you want to receive the payment directly into a hardware wallet where you control the private key. It is possible to receive the payment to a wallet via smartphone, but this is risky (the smartphone could be hacked), and when transferring that payment from the smartphone to a hardware wallet you would incur an additional fee.

Only use each Bitcoin address once, and generate a new address for every payment and every user. This helps to increase your privacy while using the network. A hardware wallet such as Trezor will allow you to generate multiple addresses controlled by multiple private keys, kept secure by a master key linked to your seed words. These addresses can be embedded into an invoice and sent out to clients as well.

If you are accepting a small number of large transactions into your business, this process works well. If you are accepting frequent and small transactions, however, say in a web shop or via e-commerce, the mechanics of this can become quite cumbersome. Copying and pasting. Making sure you don't make a mistake. Making sure that in copying the address to the computer's clipboard it isn't compromised, for example by hacking software that replaces your Bitcoin address on the clipboard with a hacker's Bitcoin address. (Double-check addresses when copying and pasting). Keeping track of payments. Making sure you got paid and noting when you got paid. Waiting for enough confirmations. All of these matters can become a real hassle when handling frequent transactions.

Fortunately, there are always people looking for new ways to implement Bitcoin. Currently one of the most useful projects for commerce is the BTCPay server. This is a self-hosted, open-source cryptocurrency payment server. The software facilitates payments from Bitcoin nodes and Lightning nodes directly to the wallets of the business or the individual.

Bitcoin is typically better for larger transactions, and Lightning is better for transactions under $25. Otherwise the transaction fee tends to be too great a proportion of the payment when transmitted via a Bitcoin node. The BTCPay server allows you to manage Bitcoin and Lightning payments, generate invoices, and run point-of-sale systems that are completely decentralized in nature.

You can set up an iPad linked to the BTCPay server and set up items for payment using pictures. So someone who is untrained can select items to allow a code to be generated for the total transaction.

You have no doubt realized by this point that there is a learning curve to comprehending what Bitcoin is about and why it is important. Hopefully this book will go some way to reducing the research required to reach this understanding. What I have given you above is just a taste of the technology that is currently available; I have no doubt the technological implementations on Bitcoin and the payment gateways will continue to improve and become more user-friendly.

My intention here is to demonstrate to you that, regardless of the logistical systems available now or in the future, you should be seriously considering accepting Bitcoin as a form of payment, either as an individual or as a business. Its ability to preserve the value of your money is unsurpassed by anything else in our modern world right now.

Given the rapidly increasing failures of our current monetary system and their potentially devastating consequences, it won't be long before many more people will start to realize what is going on. As disaster strikes, Bitcoin may well be the most logical place to run.

Are you ready, and is your business prepared, when this starts to happen?

CHAPTER SEVEN

Transformation

WHEN I HAVE watched keen Bitcoiners on YouTube try to persuade a business to accept Bitcoin as a form of payment, I often see them enthusiastically demonstrate how transferring value from one smartphone to another is ridiculously easy. Which it is. But they often don't seem to realize the larger implications of this simple transaction for businesses. To accept bitcoin, businesses currently face bookkeeping, tax, and legal hurdles. No business can start to accept Bitcoin as a form of payment unless they have given some thought to these three obstacles.

As stated previously, even though I presented the facility to pay with bitcoin for almost a year in my business, no one accepted the opportunity. So in the end I did not have to deal with these issues directly. Nonetheless, as a responsible business person I needed to be prudent, so I offer my deliberations here for those of you who may be contemplating Bitcoin as a form of payment, but have never done so before. By following my thought process, I hope you won't have to try to reinvent the wheel by yourself.

The first matter to address is how the payment itself will be recorded. Much will depend on the method you are using in order to accept the bitcoin payment in the first place. In my particular case the card machine would make a record of the payment and the staff would also make an equivalent note on the practice computer, in order to keep track of whether a client's account was in arrears.

Our computer system, for example, has a field for accepting check payments. Like most businesses we stopped accepting checks many years ago, so this field was usually redundant. This was useful as I immediately allocated this field for bitcoin payments, and we were able to customize the field to keep a record that the client had paid using bitcoin.

At the end of each month, my plan was to collate all of the payments via the computer system, to see how many bitcoin payments had been accepted in that particular time period.

Based on my experience, it is likely that other businesses interested in accepting a payment in bitcoin will receive only a trickle of payments initially, especially if they introduce it early. This is ideal as it will help them to build their recording processes gradually.

Once I had a record of my bitcoin payments, my plan was to keep a separate log of them in a parallel accounting system. This is because I used a set formatting process for my existing transactions, but planned to write the numbers differently for my Bitcoin transactions. So for clarity I wanted to keep my records separate.

At the moment accepting payments in bitcoin is rather confusing. At the time of writing this book, the value of one bitcoin is around $10,000. It is unlikely for most small retail businesses to be accepting transactions that are multiples of $10,000. As the price fluctuates around the $10,000 mark it is still fairly common for people to define the price of bitcoin in terms of a fraction of a bitcoin. An easier way to start recording these transactions may be to use units of satoshis rather than bitcoin. (Again, one hundred million satoshis equals one bitcoin.) So if someone wanted to pay for a ten-dollar item with bitcoin, they would pay one hundred thousand satoshis.

Psychologically it is easier for us humans to calculate and process whole numbers than fractions of a number. So while the transition is being made from fiat currencies to digital currencies, using satoshis as the unit of account is likely to be an easier transition than trying to record fractions of a bitcoin. By using satoshis we are calculating whole numbers, even if they are large, so it is more straightforward.

There is also something rather comforting about accepting a payment of one hundred thousand satoshis. When a loaf of bread starts going from one to ten, to one hundred dollars (or the equivalent local currency), as it does in hyperinflation, the equivalent satoshi value will be going from ten thousand to one thousand to ten. This is assuming, of course, that the price of one bitcoin would still be valued at $10,000. This dynamic demonstrates that satoshis will be buying more in the economy than the fiat currency as it is rapidly losing value.

It is highly likely that as this dynamic starts to become apparent, many people will suddenly grasp the true value of Bitcoin and the price is likely to skyrocket as more people decide they need to own some. However, Bitcoin's limited supply of 21 million units will mean that no new bitcoin can be created, making the units already in existence that much more valuable, and sending the price higher. When this happens, it will be easier to see how the transition from the old monetary system to the new monetary system is taking place before our very eyes. In this scenario, any business holding its savings in satoshis will have rapidly increasing purchasing power. These businesses will be increasing their sense of security as they watch the value go up, rather than their sense of horror as everything else rapidly changes and breaks down around them.

Once you have established the accounting practices that work best for your business, the next thing you need to consider are the tax and legal implications.

The tax requirements in each country will be very different but can of course be used by governments in order to incentivize or disincentivize their populations. Their policies will have their limits depending on other factors that may be influencing the situation. You also need to bear in mind that current governments are likely to be very protective of the existing financial system, because that is what ultimately supports their power. So if you decide to do anything that is likely to undermine this power, especially if other businesses are attempting to do the same thing at the same time, the government may well become quite aggressive in response. You'll need to handle your transformation carefully.

Many governments, including the US and the UK, are recognizing that Bitcoin is becoming very popular and as a result are updating their tax laws. At the present time, UK legislation does allow businesses to accept payments in bitcoin, but they need to keep records of such payments. The business also needs to keep records of any price rises in Bitcoin and pay the equivalent tax for any capital gain, once such bitcoin is spent or converted back to fiat. So again a potential hassle and another learning curve, but one that businesses would be wise to incorporate sooner rather than later.

This is a rapidly changing area and one that is likely to continue to change moving into the future. In many respects a financial system that uses Bitcoin as its backbone is going to change unrecognizably in the future. It is likely that many of our existing laws will be completely inappropriate if the world shifts to this new paradigm.

Many are arguing that Bitcoin cannot be adopted until the existing legal structure has been adapted in order to allow it. I would contend that the drama that is unfolding in the financial system will force the hands of governments in this respect. If an existing system is failing, the need for a replacement will eventually become urgent.

At first, in the stealth phase of a crisis when problems are not yet widely understood, governments may try to make life difficult for businesses that are accepting bitcoin. They may try to do this by increasing the tax burden on bitcoin payments to a business. I would contend that this is already happening, given the recent tax laws mentioned above which already make it awkward for a business accepting Bitcoin as a payment method.

Nevertheless, unbeknownst to most, the drama in the financial system will continue to unfold behind the scenes. Finally, one day, the system will crack suddenly, as it did in 2008, and next time it will be impossible to fix it.

As is often the case, sometimes things do not change until they absolutely have to, usually in response to a crisis. When change finally arrives, the transformation is turbulent. In such a situation just having access to an ability to pay in a different way will be life-saving.

In my own business it was my thinking that if the country should begin to enter a situation of hyperinflation, I would start offering significant discounts to those that were able to pay in bitcoin rather than fiat currency, so that eventually, in the midst of a full-blown crisis when the value of the existing currency is rapidly deteriorating, Bitcoin may well be the only form of payment I would be prepared to accept.

The more the surrounding businesses also take this approach, the harder it will be for governments to control the situation, because they can't arrest everyone—although they may try to make an example of a select few. Ultimately though, as the truth of the situation becomes more and more apparent, there will be less and less governments can do.

Many people, including politicians, fail to recognize that ultimately governments only exist because their population supports them. So as payments in bitcoin become widely popular, governments will eventually be forced to adapt and accommodate. In the meantime though, it is possible for existing authorities to make life very difficult by increasing the burdens on businesses and the burdens on the Bitcoin exchanges—all of which makes it confusing and difficult for people to adapt to a new system.

It is worth bearing in mind a couple of specific examples. Legislation is now implemented to ensure that know-your-customer (KYC) and anti-money-laundering (AML) rules are introduced on all cryptocurrency exchanges. Governments want to keep track of who is buying or selling cryptocurrencies.

In addition to being one of the best forms of money ever invented, Bitcoin is also one of the most transparent. Almost too transparent. It has allowed transactions to be followed and tracked from the day it was invented, obscuring only the knowledge of who is entering and exiting the blockchain. KYC and AML legislation facilitates this knowledge and compromises Bitcoin's privacy—as it was intended by the original creator, Satoshi Nakamoto—as a form of peer-to-peer digital cash.

There are many who are rightfully concerned about this, so there are plans to develop technology to respect the privacy of individuals while using the Bitcoin network. Current technology innovations planned for this include:

- Lightning nodes—as discussed above, they allow transactions to take place on Layer 2, separated from the Bitcoin blockchain.
- Schnorr signatures—an upgrade to the public- and private-key cryptography that currently facilitates transactions.
- Signature/key aggregation—the ability for multiple people to be responsible for signatures off-chain, as facilitated by Schnorr signature technology.
- Taproot—the ability to implement smart contracts off-chain using Schnorr signatures, but linked to the blockchain.
- Graftroot—this facilitates the transition from key aggregation to cross-input aggregation, allowing multiple people to sign for a single transaction, e.g., giving a third party access to funds in the event of death.

Some privacy can also be achieved by using "CoinJoins." A CoinJoin is a privacy-preserving technique by which multiple senders and receivers are combined within a single transaction. The goal is to make it difficult for a blockchain observer to link specific senders and receivers, thereby enabling anyone using the CoinJoin method to deny plausibly any connection with a transaction that may be tied to him or her.

There are various services that provide for CoinJoins—the most popular one currently is Wasabi Wallet. There is some debate at present about whether bitcoin that can be traced as having been through a CoinJoin could potentially lose its value by being censored—that is, because it can't be traced to its original owner. It is possible that some entities, if powerful enough, could refuse payments from CoinJoin wallets due to their lack of traceability.

Schnorr signatures and key aggregation apparently reduce the likelihood of this, as it keeps the signatures from taking place directly on the original blockchain, thereby facilitating more privacy, as they are operating on the second layer.

It is possible that governments will try to insist that businesses follow KYC and AML rules. This would increase the costs for businesses. It would also defeat the purpose of having a peer-to-peer cash system. There may be some businesses where it is in their interest to comply, but there will also be other businesses where it is not in their interest to comply. Policing such activity could be extremely difficult, if not expensive.

One of the benefits of a sound money system is that governments would need to be much more careful with their spending. They could no longer create funds out of thin air. So unlike with our current fiat money system, where money can be created for pet projects, governments would be much more answerable to the people for the things they decide to spend their money on.

Do we want more money for the NHS if it continues to exist? Or do we want to spend money making sure that businesses are tracking all of their customers by AML and KYC? I for one know which expense is likely to be more popular with the public! It is impossible for a government to continue to operate without the support of the population.

So there are two aspects to consider when it comes to tax implications. One aspect is what the tax implications are likely to be once more businesses have transitioned to a new Bitcoin world. There are also the implications while we are in that transition. Much will depend on the degree to which the government is able to maintain control as that switch is made. The inability for the government to create new money in a world that is rapidly transitioning to Bitcoin as its main means of exchange will disrupt the functions of government, undermine its power, and reduce its size. The attempt at enforced legislation, and the ensuing battle, could well be a dramatic and chaotic one.

So the dilemma for businesses right now is this: How is it possible to introduce the ability to accept bitcoin payments gradually while remaining compliant with the laws of your country? Not only to build a successful business now, but lay the groundwork for a resilient business in the future, should a financial or legislative crisis occur?

CHAPTER EIGHT

Beware

WITH THE MOVE to anything new there are always risks.[4] Bitcoin is no different. It may seem to be an exciting "catch-all" savior to our monetary problems. The truth is, that makes me a little nervous. It is almost too easy. My dental and business training taught me to consider risks. So what could we be missing here? Those in the media that wish to deride Bitcoin will happily jump on any flaw and tell you that this is why it can never work. They are either completely oblivious to its true nature and the problems it solves, or have a hidden agenda to deceive.

There *are* flaws and potential dangers in the system. It is important to be mindful of these. Clever and honest developers need to know what they might be up against. While the nefarious may take advantage of weaknesses that are pointed out to them, it is of benefit to everyone

---

4   I have included in an appendix at the end of this book of my own SWOT analysis of Bitcoin. ("SWOT" stands for "strengths, weaknesses, opportunities, and threats.") I encourage readers interested in a more granular level of detail to refer to that appendix after reading this chapter.

that we all are clear where the advantages and disadvantages are, so that the strengths can be turned into assets and weaknesses can be contained. Everyone benefits when they have the whole picture, rather than a propagandized snippet.

Bitcoin is a software protocol and many speculate about a possible breakdown of the internet. Certainly without computers Bitcoin would be useless. Our modern world is so dependent on computers these days, I suspect we would have much bigger problems to worry about if that were to happen. In reality the chances of this are fairly improbable and technological developments are constantly being worked on in order to minimize this risk, such as new satellites and radio-connected nodes. Certainly a local breakdown would be a temporary inconvenience. It is highly likely, though, that following a temporary breakdown the internet system would be re-established eventually. In such a scenario the nodes located around the world would continue to maintain the Bitcoin network.

The environmental resources expended in bitcoin mining is another major cause of concern for many. Yes the network does require a lot of power, which at the moment is increasing the longer Bitcoin continues to operate. The financial rewards associated with the operation of the network are, however, a strong incentive to keep costs down. The lower the costs the greater the profit.

Some bitcoin mining in China began because some of the hydroelectric plants were producing more energy than they could store. So someone recommended they attach a bitcoin miner to make use of the excess electricity. At least by mining bitcoin there was a financial reward associated with using this additional electricity that would not have otherwise been used.

There are also powerful incentives here for whole new methods of cheap power to be invented that could end up benefiting the entire world. All sorts of outcomes are possible, so leaping to the most catastrophic conclusion is rarely a good idea.

The power costs of Bitcoin also need to be balanced against how Bitcoin facilitates frictionless commerce. If Bitcoin becomes the easiest and most equitable means of exchange, its expenses in terms of power and effect on the environment will be easily offset by the inefficiencies in the existing financial system that it would solve. The existing paperwork and the creation of notes and coins require an equivalent, if not greater, amount of power.

Another risk that is unlikely, but possible, is an unanticipated catastrophic failure of the Bitcoin network. There are other coins that are working on different protocols that may well be able to take over if this should happen. Much would depend on whether they had been able to anticipate Bitcoin's ultimate point of failure prior to this occurring, and how well they had adapted their technology to overcome this flaw. Certainly there are compelling incentives for others to pick up on Bitcoin's weaknesses, exploit them, and promote their project as the solution. Many are already trying this, but ultimately, in this game, the majority wins. Bitcoin is streets ahead right now.

For a business, one of the biggest risks as they begin to accept payments in bitcoin is managing fluctuations in the price. These price fluctuations can be very dramatic, which is one of the reasons speculators love this asset so much. Over the ten years (so far) of Bitcoin's history, it is possible to see how the price moves in tandem with the programming of its software.

As mentioned briefly in chapter five, as a halving approaches miners start to save bitcoins rather than sell them. They know that the bitcoin supply will be reducing following the halving, but their expenses are likely to stay the same. Therefore by holding back some of their supply of bitcoin before the halving they are easing their ability to meet their expenses once the halving occurs.

This starts to reduce the supply in the system. So the flow of demand for bitcoin that was very steady approaching the halving appears to accelerate as the available supply reduces. This prompts a gradual increase in the price which speculators start to notice, prompting them to hold their investments, anticipating the inevitable price rise.

Within eighteen months of the halving, prices rise, often to a parabolic blow-off top, and the long-term holders take this as an opportunity to sell. The price then experiences a dramatic decrease and forms a bottom about one year later, usually somewhere slightly above the previous peak, before gradually rising and following the pattern all over again.

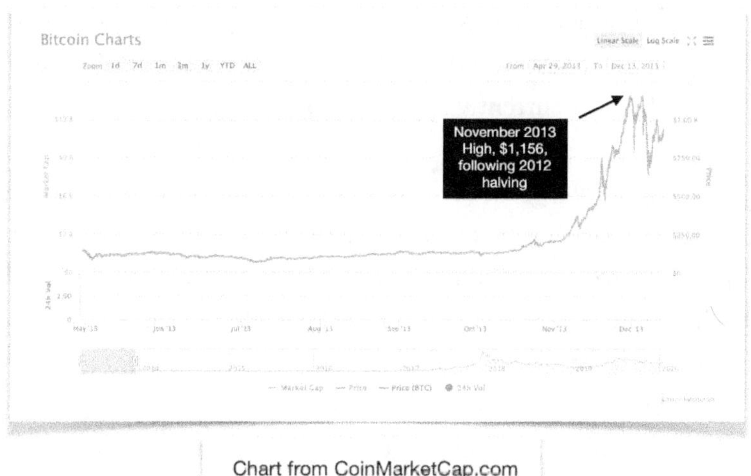

Chart from CoinMarketCap.com

This pattern is now well recognized. It has been repeated twice so far but it would be folly to rely too much on this in the future. At the moment this pattern is occurring because speculators are making money on the rise and fall in the price. However, Bitcoin was originally designed as a peer-to-peer cash system. Once Bitcoin fulfills its destiny as a means of payment in the retail sector, there will no longer be an incentive to sell once the price hits its parabolic run. This is because there will be nothing to sell it for.

When hyperinflation hits it won't be long before it is well-recognized that Bitcoin is the best form of money available on the planet. Once there is a general understanding of this, people will prefer to hold on to their bitcoin because this will be their savings and their means of paying for goods and services, particularly if the banks are about to go out of operation, or seem to be too risky.

When businesses also realize this, they will prefer to accept bitcoin for their goods and services, but will need to give their customers a strong incentive to hand them over. It may well be that they decide to offer discounted products or services to those paying in bitcoin. The level of this discount might vary depending on the fluctuations in the price and where Bitcoin currently appears to be in its price cycle.

As small businesses regain their strength by being able to operate with a currency that retains its value, the balance of power will shift to those that provide services valuable enough that people will be prepared to part with some of their savings, rather than those that just play with numbers. These being the banks, governments, and corporations. Not only this, but it will also enable fair and borderless exchange around the world, enabling the most creative and industrious to have the resources to create new innovations and solutions that are going to be required in a world that now operates on sound money.

It is worth giving thought to these solutions now. Doing so will make it less traumatic for those who are not prepared for a reality where they will struggle to care for themselves. Welfare services in a world of sound money are going to be much more reliant on charitable endeavors, with less of a safety net from the government, as it will not be able to fund these services anymore.

Many are currently excited by the rise in the price of Bitcoin over its lifetime so far, which has certainly been phenomenal and exhilarating to be a part of. This is great for those who were involved early and are now "stacking sats" ("sats" being short for "satoshis") in anticipation of their millionaire status in the future. They realize that those who own sats now will have the most purchasing power in the future.

What about those who don't own bitcoin now, though, or are born into a family where their relatives are not financially savvy? What opportunities will they have in this new Bitcoin world, where those who have bitcoin do very well, but those beginning with no resources have limited opportunity to be a part of that world? One of the main mantras of the twentieth century was social mobility. This was facilitated to a certain degree by the intervention of governments providing education and the opportunity to attend university for a low fee. How will this work in the new Bitcoin world?

The propensity for discomfort as we move from an old world to a new one is high. It will require a high degree of adaptation by the general public to shift their thinking to new ideas about how the world should really work. Many will struggle to cope and will find this very stressful.

Many have learned to rely on the government, and believe that the government should be the answer to all of their problems rather than relying on themselves. Sadly, many are unlikely to be prepared for the reality that is about to be imposed on them.

There is no doubt that life can be cruel and unfair sometimes. It can also be wonderful and rich with blessings. The existing system of economics, based on Keynesianism, has given the government an unprecedented ability, up until now, to provide safety nets for society. This has been received well by the population. Unfortunately the public doesn't realize that they have been giving away their power, gradually allowing government to take greater control of their lives. It can be comforting to rely on what you believe is a larger authority. This can often provide a source of protection from capricious elements in society. Is this a good thing though? Should individuals be shielded from the consequences of poor choices or difficult circumstances? What are the unintended outcomes of such a measure?

If people know they can rely on the government or an insurance company to provide something like health care, what incentive do they have to take care of themselves and ensure they never need it? It is unpopular to voice this, but there are plenty of people willing to take advantage of anything offered to them for free, and many who will exploit and game a system that has primarily been designed to help others, often to the detriment of those it was designed to help in the first place. This can be a very difficult thing to police, with political landmines everywhere you step if you try to address the issue.

At the beginning of the twentieth century there were great divides between the rich and the poor. The owners and the workers. Perhaps we needed the dramas at the beginning of that century to shake up the system, to give us the opportunity to break some of the old paradigms. Maybe it was necessary to create the illusion, by inflating the monetary system, of a very prosperous, almost equal society, in order to free our minds enough to create a new and fairer system. It hasn't worked though. The resulting equality is a myth, with interest rates and tax burdens completely out of proportion to each other for different elements of society.

The time has come to end the party. A new structure is on the horizon which will demand a greater sense of responsibility.

A system of sound money only rewards those able to provide goods and services. Those who aren't able to do this are more likely to be rejected by society. Those whose value is not appreciated by others may have a very difficult time.

Close to where I currently live, the first workhouse was built and developed in 1824, by the Reverend John T. Becher and George Nicholls. At the time the destitute were the responsibility of the local parish and it was a constant problem. Many of these workhouses nurtured a very harsh environment as a disincentive for people to go there. This was very effective and many of these workhouses survived in the UK well into the 1960s. For many they were a living nightmare. I have heard reports of older people living in absolute fear of having to go to the workhouse, that fear never leaving them for their entire lives.

Younger generations have been fortunate to grow up in a time when they did not need to fear this. However, as a new monetary system is born, this will change. New ideas will be needed to support those unwilling or unable to support themselves. Hopefully our newfound compassion, as a result of experiencing a welfare system, will stimulate our creativity to come up with something better than a workhouse. This will likely depend on the payoffs and rewards for those instituting new systems.

For a few decades, many of us in the west have been protected from harsh realities to some extent. The cost is the impending destruction of our existing financial system, with insurmountable debt that can never be paid off. When the existing system cracks, those who can will run for safety. The path of least resistance could well be Bitcoin. But what are the ultimate consequences of this, and are we prepared for them?

In times past, social structures served to keep society ordered. The unwritten, often unexpressed, social rules helped everyone to know their place and offered some sense of security to the population. Previous writers show us that social structures could often be very constraining and suffocating. Certainly it would appear that parts of the world were longing for a change from this, and the ability to be more flexible in their lifestyles.

The changes in the twentieth century appear to have achieved this, but at what cost? The unrestrained freedom has led to breakdowns in the rules for interpersonal relationships and the ways in which families interact with each other. Families are now less likely to care for the elderly, and partners are less likely to be loyal to each other. Society accepts all of this as an opportunity for unbridled freedom. The hidden cost is anxiety, mental anguish, and broken hearts. Lonely old—and young—people who have no idea what the future holds, or feel that it has been stolen from them. From this perspective many appear to have paid a high price for their freedom. Is this reality really in our best interests?

Finally, what about the dangers of having all of our transactions monitored on an open ledger? The media are keen to tell us that only drug dealers and criminals use this technology. In reality, any criminal relying on Bitcoin is much more likely to be traced, as all of the transactions throughout Bitcoin's history can currently be tracked and linked to individuals when buying or selling on exchanges. Many think that this doesn't matter. If they aren't a criminal they have nothing to hide. In truth, how many of us are just steps away from being a criminal, once a new law is introduced that makes it so? Laws that at this moment in time are impossible to predict?

Certainly, in a world where governments hold enough power, having the world's finances operating on a blockchain controlled by a central entity is very dangerous. At least with Bitcoin as a *decentralized* blockchain, this power is disrupted, limiting the supply of bitcoin and thereby controlling Bitcoin's value. Any world that operates using this technology as a base layer will disrupt the control of a central entity by removing its ability to issue money at its command.

It still, however, gives those with the most resources the ability to analyze the blockchain. In doing so it allows them privileged access to knowledge that it is difficult for the average person to take advantage of. How many people truly understand the dangers of this?

We have time to consider the answers to these questions. The almost inevitable—though not guaranteed—path to a new Bitcoin world is likely to be a rocky one. Bitcoin as a technology is still incredibly new and it is still possible that something could happen to disrupt its trajectory. Although that does leave me wondering what our fate would be if this happens…

When?
The Future

CHAPTER NINE

Systems, Corruption, and the NHS

TODAY WE FIND ourselves in some difficulty. New laws are being made every day to try to neutralize the effects of corruption at the core. It's not working. Along with the rapidly increasing digits in our financial system, laws are growing at an exponential rate in an effort to contain the resulting problems.

Natural laws are known by the heart, but man-made laws are processed by the head. As the head decisions increasingly diverge from the heart decisions, human beings become confused. Faced with the threat of an authority figure, they will ignore the heart entirely.

Stanley Milgram wrote of this in 1963, in the *Journal of Abnormal and Social Psychology*. In the article, he explained how he had conducted a series of experiments to test the subjects' obedience to authority. He found, unexpectedly, that a high proportion of the participants would fully, albeit reluctantly, obey all instructions.

The experiment participants were encouraged to turn up the dial on an electric chair and administer a shock to unseen participants if they failed to answer a series of questions correctly. (The unseen participants were actors; despite their repeated pleas and realistic shrieks that mimicked the approach of death, no shocks were actually administered.) Despite these very convincing performances, the large majority of participants continued to increase the dial. Some of the participants protested and told the experimenter that they didn't want to continue. The scientist conducting the experiment, in an authoritarian white coat, was unsympathetic, telling the participants that they needed to continue for the sake of the experiment. So they did.

Confused people make bad choices.

Some confused people become politicians, striving to please the public at all costs. Without the approval of the public they lose their position at the next election. Or they might not achieve the privileges of power they would be entitled to if they were elected into government.

The public constantly want more money for schools and health. To satisfy this demand, in the 1990s the government in the UK started entering into public-private partnerships (known as PPPs) to help fund these projects, specifically to help build schools and hospitals. The government's existing budgets didn't allow for the investment that was necessary for their favorite promises to the public. By partnering with private firms the government hoped to fund these projects more easily and work around their budget constraints.

The result was massively profitable for the private companies. The governments, however, not only in the UK but in other countries around the world that copied the idea, ended up burdened with even more debt than they had before. Not only this, but their continuing poor management has resulted in ever-increasing errors when it comes to handling the resources of others.

Confused politicians make bad choices. By virtue of their position, they can also make bad laws.

Consider the implications, then, of the emergence of a new way to program rules into software that can't be changed, a future in which politicians' corrupt rules are enforced on an incorruptible system: the blockchain. This groundbreaking innovation, introduced to the world by Satoshi Nakamoto, has limitless applications. Governments around the world are now becoming aware of this—they can repurpose the ideas behind a blockchain for their own devices.

It turns out that immutable ledgers can be very useful things, particularly when organizations around the world rely on paper trails in order to verify transactions, ensure legal compliance, and track ownership of property other than just money. Legal agreements are finalized using contracts. It is now possible for some of these contracts to be programmed onto the immutable ledger of a blockchain, depending on the software model used. This kind of digital contract is known as a "smart contract."

At the moment the Ethereum blockchain is best known for smart contracts, although as previously mentioned, software updates are planned for Bitcoin to allow smart contracts to take place on the Bitcoin blockchain as well.

Contracts are tricky things. They don't always work out the way you intended and sometimes, due to unfortunate outcomes, they need to be re-thought and re-written. Our ideas about how our society should evolve is also being constantly re-thought and re-considered all of the time. The problem with immutable ledgers for this kind of agreement is that they are by design immutable—that is, unable to be changed.

If our society is operating in an unhealthy way, programming existing rules and regulations onto a protocol that can't be changed seems to me to be a recipe for disaster. Not only this, but central banks, corporations, and governments designing their own immutable ledgers to carry business procedures, laws, and a national currency that can be infinitely inflated when convenient for them, without the population having any control or say in such management, is asking for the quality of lives for the majority to disappear into oblivion, as the current dysfunction of our existing monetary system will continue unabated.

Sadly, the promise of a welfare system can be a powerful incentive to dupe a population into accepting what a government would like to sell them. The implications of this are important to understand, so I am sharing here some of the insights that I have gleaned during my professional career to demonstrate the issues a bit more clearly.

The National Health Service (NHS) is now almost a religion in the UK, cultivated by the news media regularly featuring stories of individuals whose lives have benefitted as a result of the NHS, in an effort to convince us how lucky we are that we live in a country where this is available to us.

Please don't misunderstand me, many good things have come about as a result of the NHS, especially in the early years. It is no coincidence, however, that its growth has corresponded with the growth in our fiat monetary system. Welfare services were a major promise to the veterans of the two world wars, and as the financial numbers had to be fudged to pay for the wars, why not fudge them to pay for welfare services as well? Everyone wins!

The trouble with health care and other welfare services is that they are such an emotive topic, and different people have varying ideas as to what should be available under a universal health-care system.

A perilous dilemma as we start to consider immutable rules is that a centrally managed health-care system could start to dictate what is best for the population it is serving, even if it does not always result in the best outcome, or conflicts with the hearts of individuals, as was experienced by my mother and our family. As these conflicts escalate and the population protests, drawing boundaries for politicians becomes very difficult, so the system grows to an unimaginable size—not only problematic to operate, but also to fund.

As the costs start to grow unreasonably, an attempt is usually made to control them, but in an environment that is managed by politicians influenced by popular opinion, the wisest choices aren't always made. The most expedient option is usually to place a limit on what can be provided by a service, which doesn't always have an immediate negative outcome, but in the fullness of time, as the effects play out, it ends up having a direct effect on the morale of staff. The equipment and materials that can be provided are eventually compromised as old things wear out and are not replaced, so the quality of the service suffers. Everyone starts to complain about this, so rules are made to improve the quality without providing the required resources, placing unsustainable pressure on the service providers.

The problems creep up slowly and stealthily. Dentistry and other kinds of health care are complex professions to be in, even if you are only focusing on the health-care aspects, but most health professionals now have to cope with all of these extraneous issues of broken systems as well, none of which they signed up for when they joined the profession, and all of which they are now powerless to fix because most of them now operate in the centralized organization of the NHS. I am aware of other professionals who have been my patients—such as solicitors, bankers, judges, and policemen—that are experiencing similar issues in their professions as well. This is symptomatic, I believe, of the financial pressures and compromises that have built up over decades behind the scenes.

It is a situation that for many becomes more and more unreasonable to handle, especially if they are concerned about the integrity of the service that they are providing. Some, due to the commitments and obligations they are surrounded by, do not have time to investigate the bigger problems.

When offering a product or service, price is everything, and usually the only means a business has to increase its revenues and cover its expenses. The ability to establish and control prices is the feature of a business that has become a monopoly. In the private sector there are laws that try to prevent this. For example, a merger between the supermarkets Sainsbury's and Asda was recently thwarted by the UK government. This is because monopolies distort free markets by becoming so large that they attain the powerful ability to set prices either up or down, depending on their agenda. This puts their customers at a disadvantage. They are at the mercy of what this business chooses to charge them. They cannot choose to go anywhere else. There is nowhere else to go, because no one else can afford to compete.

In health care the NHS in the UK is a monopoly, but one run by the government. This is because as the major provider of medical and dental health care, it can set the prices. Medical health care is free at the point of demand, but any dentist agreeing to provide NHS dental services has to agree to charge only the fees set by the government. This eliminates competition and centralizes control of the system, eventually reducing innovation and creativity in that organization, but also making it very expensive for other businesses to compete.

In the UK it was only when the price-versus-quality dynamic in dental health care became bad enough that patients were prepared to seek out and pay for better services, although they then had to pay significant premiums to do so. Once I was established working in the private sector, I would attract patients who had many nightmare stories to tell of their history with dentists. Many of them were terrified as a result of their previous trials. They often had serious problems in their mouths as a consequence too: an inevitable outcome of a service that cannot sustain the quality of its provision.

I would sometimes attend dental conferences in America. Invariably, if I found myself sitting next to an American dentist, they would ask me, "Why are British teeth so bad?" I could lecture them for days on this subject to give them the ins and outs. Instead I would simply say—the NHS.

The trouble with one large entity being responsible for a service is that it allows it to take the attitude, "Our way or the highway." This is problematic when there is no other highway to go to. Not only this, but that highway is riddled with problems as it figures out how it is going to build it. The bigger it gets the more immovable it is too.

New ideas are lost in a miasma of groupthink as those at the top of the chain attempt to protect their self-interests, while everyone below them clearly doesn't know enough to challenge their flawed ideas, even if they do. The newly flawed ideas then become institutionalized in concepts (through centrally funded science projects) that no one without the appropriate resources can challenge. These are then sold to their colleagues, the public, and the legal system as in their best interests, because now their ideas are "evidence-based."

These are the problems with large institutionalized systems. Human beings are flawed and will make mistakes at every level. But when there is no room to maneuver away from those mistakes, it becomes a problem. Large institutions have their advantages, sure, but the problems are more problematic, particularly once everyone has come to depend on them.

What happens when all of this dysfunction is programmed onto a blockchain?

It took me some time to understand that the way the NHS is organized and funded—the lack of flexibility in the system and the difficulties experienced when trying to compete with it—is a big problem. It was only as I grappled with these dilemmas in my own career, as I decided to set up my own business as a way out of the nightmare, that I was then confronted with the problems in the financial system. This was powerfully brought home to me by the financial crisis in 2008.

Understanding the financial world was, to me, the final piece of the puzzle. It enabled me to understand how the funding was achieved to set up the NHS in the first place. Without the ability of the government to manipulate the nation's finances, beginning after the First World War, it would not have been possible.

By centralizing the system, the government has stolen from trained professionals the opportunity to provide the services they know are likely to be best for their clients, and the ability of these professionals to challenge the thinking of the authorities and re-imagine new health-care solutions based on their experience.

In the UK, we now find ourselves in a situation where the health-care system is costing more and more while getting worse and worse. No one understands why. In an effort to solve the problem, people protest, petition, and vote for the person who promises to provide more money, never realizing that it is the money that got us into this mess in the first place.

The situation is out of balance. In an effort to restore that balance the politicians use the only tool they have: Make a new law! Even if those new laws in the context of the foundation are utterly crazy!

Many of us are terrified of these laws, afraid of the consequences of breaking them, whether it's a fine that creates chaos financially or actual jail time. We do everything we can to avoid breaking them, but as a result we find our options more and more constrained. Finally there is nowhere to turn, like sheep cornered in a pen. This is troubling and confusing for those of us caught up in this dynamic, having no idea what is going on.

Too many of our rules are suffocating society and are being generated to counteract problems that have occurred at the financial core. This has created a sickness in our society that I believe won't be healed until our money is honest again.

CHAPTER TEN

Digital Prisons

WHILE THE BITCOIN protocol implements changes through consensus due to its decentralized structure, a blockchain run by a government or a corporation will be programmed and controlled by these central entities, and as a result they will have the final say on any changes that may or may not be made to the software protocols running their blockchains.

When they have finalized their plans, do we want to accept enthusiastically what these central entities are offering us? Or will we choose another path?

At the core of this issue is self-sovereignty. To what extent are we willing to take responsibility for our future and choose to use the most effective mechanism for encompassing this? Alternatively, do we want to continue to delegate our power to the government, believing that it can take care of us and fix all of our problems even though the system is really set up to fulfill its own agendas?

Not only can the blockchain be used to execute smart contracts, it can also be used to manage data: to keep track of and transfer property rights in the real estate market or to keep tabs on medical records, to offer just two examples.

Privacy, as mentioned earlier, is an ongoing topic of debate in the cryptocurrency world. Some argue that everything should be transparent so that we can capture the data of all of the criminals, including the ones who might have power in government. This conveniently overlooks the imbalance of power between an individual to check the behavior of a government, and the far greater power of a government to check the behavior of an individual.

Others argue that privacy is a basic human right. I am inclined to agree with this, because if someone else has the ability to access knowledge that is personal to you, it does give them the ability to manipulate you, particularly, as I just mentioned, if there is an imbalance of power in the ability of the parties involved to access that knowledge. This can be demonstrated by looking into the concept of game theory.

Game theory is an interesting area of study. As I became interested in the blockchain space I started to hear about it frequently, so I decided to look into it more comprehensively.

Game theory analyzes the strategic interaction among rational decision makers—that is, those who are in a dilemma and the decisions they make to resolve that dilemma. There are serious intellectuals with significant resources who build mathematical models in order to analyze the "games" associated with game theory.

If you would like to learn more about this in an easily digestible way I can recommend a TV series called *The Liar Game* that was produced in Japan in 2007, which dramatizes a number of these games. Watching this series made me realize how manipulative game theory can be—those that set up the game have all the information and so can effectively predict or manage the outcome, while the participants are usually left in confusion as blind actors in the game.

Game theory has multiple applications. It can be used in

- human and animal behavior,
- economic behavior,
- political science,
- biology,
- computer science and logic,
- philosophy,
- and interactive epistemology—what it means for the collective to have common beliefs and knowledge.

In thinking about this you start to realize that people can use game theory extremely widely, particularly when these game theory models are based on mathematical data. A game applied to interactive epistemology, for example, studies how likely it is that a population will overthrow the king. Who would be interested in that I wonder—hmm?

Perhaps understanding the power of this, a government wants to build a model of the behavior of its population. To do so, it needs one essential element: *data*. It doesn't even need a complete data set. It can extrapolate quite interesting predictions just from samples of the data. *It doesn't need all of it.* Anyone who has studied game theory is patently aware of this.

We need to consider this. Although we might be encouraged to protect our personal data as individuals, the danger here could be much broader than that. Just by being part of an interconnected network, we will be providing valuable information to anyone analyzing that collective data, whether we are protecting our own personal data or not.

In some respects we already live in this world—most of our activities are occurring more and more frequently over the internet and social media. This provides multitudes of data for those that wish to analyze it. It also provides scope for manipulation as well.

This was illustrated with the Cambridge Analytica scandal after the Trump election in 2016. Swathes of personal data had apparently been sold by Facebook to Cambridge Analytica. This allowed them to analyze the data on people's social media feeds, and then, based on what they discovered, target messaging back to social media that would influence the election in the way they wanted. Apparently.

Regardless of the details we were given through the media, the fact that it was possible for Facebook to do this, and that there are whole companies that buy this information, was a revelation. What do you suppose they are buying it for? Why do you think so much on the internet is free? This data is valuable. Not just because of the individuals it can target, but because of the knowledge it delivers about a population when analyzed properly. We don't have the first idea how valuable that data really is and how the knowledge it provides could be dangerous to us in the future.

These are the battles we are facing at the moment. How much more dangerous could they be when all of our finances and laws also operate on a blockchain? Blockchains that can monitor our whereabouts and potentially punish us without recourse. That make automatic withdrawals from our digital accounts. That fine us for the slightest misdemeanor when we don't comply with the rules the powers-that-be have established on the blockchain.

We stand on the brink of a dangerous precipice…

China has long been a champion of social monitoring. Facial recognition software is now regularly being used to monitor the activities of the public as they go about their daily lives. Misdemeanors caught on camera, like jaywalking, are automatically added to the public record. If required, fines are applied to the citizens' centrally held credit score. Credit scores are taken into account increasingly, for example when applying for a job, travelling, or even when attempting to secure the best education for their children. The long-term implications of this are terrifying.

The Chinese president, Xi Jinping, has recently endorsed blockchain technology, declaring it "an important breakthrough" and saying that China would "seize the opportunity." Hmm, for what I wonder? Over five hundred blockchain projects from many of China's most powerful companies have already registered with China's Cyberspace Administration.

You may still be operating under the illusion that governments are trustworthy; perhaps you think this isn't your problem. Don't become too complacent. The UK government is also currently looking very seriously into the application of blockchain technology.

The areas it has identified that would benefit from the blockchain are all areas that currently require massive administration teams.

Examples include

- Health care,
- Work and pensions,
- Intellectual property rights,
- Tax and internal revenue monitoring,
- National identity management systems,
- Justice and tribunal services,
- Post-Brexit border control of trade,
- Land registration of property,
- Grants and student loans,
- Public procurement,
- Voting and democracy,
- Secure banking services,
- Education and skills,
- Sport.

This all sounds very exciting for those involved with the new technology. I, however, stand aghast, thinking of all the flawed rules, created by a flawed society, that are about to be enforced through the use of immutable ledgers.

The banks aren't immune to the appeal of this either. The International Monetary Fund (IMF), the European Central Bank (ECB), and the Bank of England are all now talking about how cryptocurrencies are the future. Their own cryptocurrencies, that is—not Bitcoin.

Bitcoin, much to the chagrin of banks everywhere, places constraints on their ability to create new money, as they have been doing for the past one hundred years. So the technology needs to be repurposed for their own ends. While they now agree that it is possible to have a form of money programmed into software, they want *their own* software to use. *That they can control.*

Bitcoin won't do because they can't control that. So it needs to be reinvented as The Blockchain. In the hands of these organizations, however, The Blockchain is nothing more than a glorified Excel spreadsheet that they have a backdoor to. It solidifies their existing corrupt paradigms, financial and otherwise, onto a system that is designed to be changeable only when it suits them.

The cryptocurrency speculators, however, will not be moved to anything other than giddiness as their favorite token scales the heights on the exchanges. If they are lucky they will sell it quickly before the price crashes again. They will then scour the internet looking for the next pet project to pump and dump, promoting each coin's worthiness as "Our next vehicle to the future!"

Those that define anything other than Bitcoin as a "sh*t coin" may have a point. In the wrong hands, blockchain is nothing more than a vastly efficient tool for corruption and the means for building a digital prison.

CHAPTER ELEVEN

Prophecy

WHEN CONSIDERING ADOPTING anything new it is wise to consider the future. There are those that will use analytical tools to try to predict what is likely to happen, like traders that use technical analysis in financial markets, insurance companies that employ actuaries to ensure that they are making sensible future choices for the company finances, and other companies that make use of game theory and big-data analysis technology. All of these methods try to predict future outcomes based on behaviors that have been studied in the past.

For those that don't have the intelligence or the resources for these methods, though, they will often resort to other means, relying on their own intuition or sometimes consulting psychics and mystics. Prophecy is also a tool—often a fascinating one—that is used. It can give us ideas about the future and allow us to consider and test these ideas in our minds, imagining the possible outcomes we would like to see or not see.

I had a religious upbringing. Every Sunday my family would attend church and every evening the family would sit in a group, share what had happened during their day,and then say prayers together before bed. Reading the Bible was part of this ritual, so growing up I was very familiar with the Bible and its stories.

The Bible is full of prophecy. Much of the Old Testament is a lead-up to the New Testament and the predictions of a coming savior. The last book of the Bible in the New Testament is the book of Revelation, a book of predictions about the future. St. John, the author of the book, describes the visions he receives while staying on the island of Patmos in the Aegean Sea.

The story is not comforting. It outlines the coming apocalypse and the disasters leading up to it. Many scholars and historians have puzzled over Revelation for centuries, wondering what it could mean.

As blockchain technology reaches into the public consciousness, many who are enamored by prophecy exclaim in horror about The Mark of the Beast and the predictions surrounding it. Their concern comes from Revelation 13:16–17, in the King James Version (KJV), a translation of the Bible from the 1600s:

> [16]And he causeth all, both small and great, rich
> and poor, free and bond, to receive a mark in
> their right hand, or in their foreheads:

> [17]And that no man might buy or sell, save he
> that had the mark, or the name of the beast, or
> the number of his name.

Reading the book of Revelation in my youth, I too was concerned by the drama of the story. I had no idea what that mark might be. Thirty years later, however, it is becoming apparent how the predictions in Revelation could be evolving into reality.

Is it possible that all of us could be forced to accept a chip in our hands, with which a government-enforced digital blockchain token is the only allowed means of payment? This future is now a distinct possibility. I was recently at a conference in Germany where a delegate proudly announced to the other delegates that she had now had a chip implanted in her hand and that there was really nothing to worry about with it. Oh dear!

There are now employees who have these chips implanted if they are to work for a particular company, as the chip allows them to get in and out of the building and into any restricted areas that they may need access to in the course of their work.

George Orwell, in his book *1984*, wrote about the ultimate outcomes for a heavily surveilled society. This book still tells the most terrifying story I have ever read. It outlines a dystopian nightmare: a government that surrounds the population with hidden cameras, tortures those unwilling to comply, in order to reeducate them, and issues propaganda to the population in the form of "doublespeak."

Interesting that his book was written in the 1940s. How did he know? Televisions had been invented, but iPhones were still a pipe dream then! It is almost as if he wrote it as a warning to us, of how this surveillance society could play out. Maybe he was communicating to us someone else's idea of what is intended for humanity. Given the prediction in Revelation 13:16-17, is it possible that there are those that can plan such things?

We live in a society where we believe we have some say in the outcome of our destiny by voting and petitioning our politicians. How much power, though, does that really give any of us?

There is a quote, normally attributed to the German banker Mayer Amschel Rothschild, that is worth considering: "Give me control of a nation's money and I care not who makes its laws."

Regardless of where the quote comes from, the message it delivers is a powerful one: It suggests that if you have enough money, you would have the resources to bribe or corrupt any person or organization who is responsible for upholding the law, particularly if you could make that person's or organization's circumstances very difficult, if not impossible, for failing to follow your wishes. What if someone like this had enough money to write their own laws and have them widely accepted by the public?

Now, I am going to enter some tricky territory here and possibly lose many of my readers, but I think it is incredibly important that in these dangerous times we explore all ideas—even those we would rather not look at—in order to get a complete picture of what we could be dealing with here, as humanity makes an important choice as to the next stages of its future.

Some of the information I am going to share with you has been dismissed as conspiracy theory and completely derided. It may well be that most of the following is nonsense, but many people take these ideas very seriously. As a result, I think it is important to include them in the conversation.

Author and researcher David Wilcock has written a book, freely available on the internet, called *Financial Tyranny: Defeating the Greatest Cover-Up of All Time*.[5] While I disagree with the solutions outlined in the book, it does a fairly good job of outlining the unreasonableness of the existing financial system and how corrupt it has become.

In exploring this, David's book gives a very detailed analysis of the history of secret societies.[6] David explains that when the world was dogmatically ruled by the church, in the past, many that felt oppressed by this turned to Masonry.

It would appear that human beings will always find a way out of oppressive structures from which no way out is designed, even if it means they end up jumping from the frying pan into the fire. Those that believe that removing one kind of tyranny means that you don't get another should read *Animal Farm*, by George Orwell as well.

According to David's book, at the highest degrees of Masonry it is revealed to participants that Lucifer is the one holding the light and hidden knowledge. Lower levels of Masonry are kept from knowing this until they have gradually proved themselves worthy. New members at the lower levels are recruited from existing religious backgrounds, because they have demonstrated their keenness to buy into a belief system.

---

5 https://divinecosmos.com/davids-blog/1023-financial-tyranny/
6 *New World Order: the Ancient Plan of Secret Societies*, by William T. Still

Once established as members, their beliefs are gradually turned. They are encouraged to prove themselves as they move up each level by making secret oaths. They are tempted with rewards of increased influence and resources for doing so. Anyone who has taken an oath of secrecy and is then brave enough to attempt to reveal the secrets of Masonry are subjected to the most dire punishments.

While elements of the Christian church could be interpreted as dark, repurposing Satan as a savior seems like a bit of a stretch. Keeping this knowledge hidden from lower-level Masons until they pass their initiations at the higher levels appears to be a rather sinister form of trickery.

Using the power of fear and secrecy, the Masonic lodges have apparently been able gradually to capture key seats of influence and power around the world, with a secret master plan to ensure that their ultimate agenda can be put into place. Many prominent politicians in their public speeches have been heard to refer to this New World Order.

What if the organizers of the Masons, with their focus on becoming wealthy, and then gaining footholds in power, were able to manipulate the laws of countries, and the implementation of justice, to their own ends?

Certainly, with the way these systems are currently set up, it would be possible to do this. If the entire system of finance and law is managed by rules, all you need to do is gradually tweak the rules from a powerful enough position in order to establish your own agenda.

Any system that operates from the top down has the potential to be corrupted. Successful organizations require honorable leaders that keep the well-being of the collective in mind. Any organization, whether it be a church, a government, or a secret society, that strays from this will descend into destruction and chaos.

It would appear that the Masons have had some interesting influences in their history.

David reports on another book, by William Guy Carr,[7] who alleges that in 1773 Mayer Rothschild convened a meeting of twelve other wealthy men at his home in Frankfurt.

At this meeting they created a twenty-five-point strategy for a new group called The Illuminati, with which they intended to infiltrate Freemasonry.

A document outlining the strategy was discovered when one of their couriers was struck by lightning while carrying it. The authorities, on examining the belongings of this man, discovered it. And so it came to light.

David's book lists the points in this document that he felt were most shocking, and I list them here also. Their strategies included the following:

> #1. Use violence and terrorism rather than academic discussions...
> #4. Any and all means were justified, on the grounds that a moral code left a politician vulnerable...

---

7   *Pawns in the Game*, by William Guy Carr

#6. Remain invisible until the very moment when it has gained such strength that no cunning or force can undermine it...

#7. Use mob psychology to control the masses. "Without absolute despotism" one cannot rule efficiently.

#8. Advocate the use of alcoholic liquors, drugs, moral corruption, and all forms of vice, used systematically by "agenteurs" to corrupt the youth.

#9. Seize property by any means and without hesitation, to secure submission and sovereignty.

#10. Foment wars, but direct the peace conferences so that neither of the combatants gains territory. They would be placed further in debt and therefore into our power.

#12. Choose candidates for public office who will be servile and obedient to our commands, so they may be readily used as PAWNS IN OUR GAME.

#13. Use the Press for propaganda to control all outlets of public information, while remaining in the shadows, clear of blame.

#14. Make the masses believe they have been the prey of criminals. Then restore order to appear as the saviors.

#15. Create financial panics; use hunger to subjugate the masses.

#16. Infiltrate Freemasonry... "When the hour strikes for our sovereign Lord of all the World to be crowned, these same hands will sweep away everything that might stand in his way."...

#18. A Reign of Terror is the most economical way to bring about speedy subjection.

#19. Masquerade as political, financial, and economic advisers to carry out our mandates... without fear of exposing "the secret power behind national and international affairs."

> #20. ULTIMATE WORLD GOVERNMENT is the goal. It will be necessary to establish huge monopolies, so even the largest fortunes... [will] go to the bottom together with the credit of their governments ON THE DAY AFTER THE GREAT POLITICAL SMASH.
>
> #21. Economic War. Rob the Goyim (nations) of their landed properties and industries with a combination of high taxes and unfair competition.
>
> #22. Make the Goyim destroy each other so there will only be the proletariat [poor] left in the world, with a few millionaires devoted to our cause, and sufficient police and soldiers to protect our interest.
>
> #23. Call it THE NEW ORDER. Appoint a Dictator...

Nice.

Now you may think that 1773 is a long time ago, and that these ideas diminished with time.

There are other authors who write similarly, however. David Icke exposes the Ultra Zionists and their core death cult secret society, known as the Sabbatean-Frankists.[8] I won't go into further detail about that here—if you are interested I will let you do your own research.

If any of the above is true, it would appear that humanity could have some formidable enemies that are hateful, have significant resources, and intend to exploit governments and other powerful organizations for their own ends. The most unsettling thing about them is how secretive and manipulative they are. While I believe individual

---

8   *The Trigger,* by David Icke

privacy to be a human right, collective secrecy is sinister because of the imbalance in the power dynamic that leads to the vulnerability of individuals.

If you believe these organizations exist, is it possible that they are organized and secretive enough to build their own digital currencies with their own blockchains, selling them to humanity as corporate or government coins? As replacements for a corrupt, worthless dollar and other fiat currencies as they finally break down irretrievably?

Manipulative enough to eliminate cash, forcing everyone into a cashless society, with a microchip placed in their hands and a central ledger that keeps a record of all financial transactions?

Powerful enough to analyze the movements of the population from data generated by the blockchain? To use game theory to maneuver the citizenry into a sophisticated pen from which their ultimate plan can be instituted?

It may sound far-fetched, but if you were designing an evil plan to lock down humanity and bring it under your control, wouldn't this be a pretty effective blueprint?

If you could pull it off…

CHAPTER TWELVE

Bitcoin Fixes This

SOME SAY THAT "Money is the root of all evil." I know this is a misquote from the Bible, but I believe at this point that shortened definition absolutely applies. The corruption of our money by basing it on flawed "rules" has allowed its quality to devalue. This has set the stage for a downward spiral of degeneration in society, managed by the application of increasingly draconian laws. It has allowed resources to gravitate unfairly to expensive wars and given unprecedented advantages to unequal ends of society, while the rest of the population has been left bread crumbs in terms of a now-deteriorating welfare system.

It is time to turn the tide.

The most valuable talents that human beings have are their limitless creativity, and their desire to pursue that which is most likely to achieve their highest good and the good of others. They can often end up solving problems they didn't even know they had.

Or maybe they did know they had?

Bitcoin is a remarkable invention. Unlike the copycat blockchain companies that governments are currently so keen to invest in, Bitcoin has some distinguishing features that currently make it a superior technology in terms of its benefits for humanity. It is an excellent vehicle for escaping treacherous intentions that may have been planned for us.

As a result of the network of nodes, Bitcoin is decentralized, meaning that it can never be shut down or censored or controlled by a single individual, such as a dictator.

It is a blockchain that is fully and publicly auditable. So unlike a secret society network, this is a network that is kept open and transparent. Anyone can analyze the software and see how it is designed to work.

Changes can only be made via a consensus of agreement using the validation provided by a rare number supplied by the miners. This makes fraud very costly. New software will only be implemented via agreements with the nodes. The actions of the developers, and the new protocols they suggest, are kept in check by the users through its transparent software.

Unlike a government-issued token, which is likely to be continuously inflated using the arguments of Keynesian economics, bitcoin cannot be inflated. Since its supply is limited, its quality as a form of money is protected, because no one entity can change it. Everyone knows how many there are. One bitcoin will always be one bitcoin, and there will never be more than 21 million bitcoins in existence. Its value in relation to dollars or other fiat currencies only changes due to the number of participants on the network and the ever-increasing amounts of fiat currency being created by the financial system.

Imagine the game of Monopoly I discussed in chapter two, with all of that extra paper money that was introduced into the game. Now imagine that someone comes along with an entirely new set of banknotes. Eventually this new set of banknotes will be the only ones that can be played with, but the players vary in their ability to catch on to this. So when it comes to paying rent, they have a choice: continue paying rent using the old money, or use the new money? Accept the new money as rent, or only accept the old money?

Those that are smart will continue to pay rent for as long as possible with the old money, but will negotiate with their tenants and incentivize them to pay in the new money, thereby starting to collect this new money, ready for the time when this new form of transaction will be the only money that is accepted.

The ones that adopt this strategy first will be the ones with the advantage when all of the old money is no longer circulating in the game. Everyone will start to realize and adopt the same strategy. No one will want the old money anymore.

The only problem is, while this maneuver is being played out, all of the players are being persuaded that a myriad of different banknotes might be the ones that are eventually the new note, the only one that can be used. Each new currency will have a very different outcome for the game, and sorting out which one will be the winner will be the key not only to coming out the victor, but determining how satisfying the endgame ultimately is.

Once the transition has fully been made to the new money, however, especially if one limited in supply has been chosen, the game will start to function as it did previously, when there was an initial limited supply of bank money. The transition, however, will give the previous losing participants a chance to redress the balance with the previous property owners who had been dominating the game before the extra paper money was introduced.

Playing this game will not prevent some from winning, or others from losing. Life is inherently unequal and while we rely on money as a way of exchanging value with each other, there will always be those with more and others with less. But at least when we are using sound money there is the opportunity to play a game that is more balanced, so that those that produce goods and services that help others are rewarded, rather than the system that we have now that rewards those that are rent-seeking and best able to manipulate numbers.

This is where we now find ourselves in the real world in 2019. Billions of dollars are currently being fed into the financial markets behind the scenes via repurchase agreements (commonly known as the "repo market") by the Federal Reserve in the US, in order to stabilize the financial markets on the brink of a crisis. This is a sign of big trouble, as a similar dynamic set off the financial crisis of 2008. Something could be about to break.

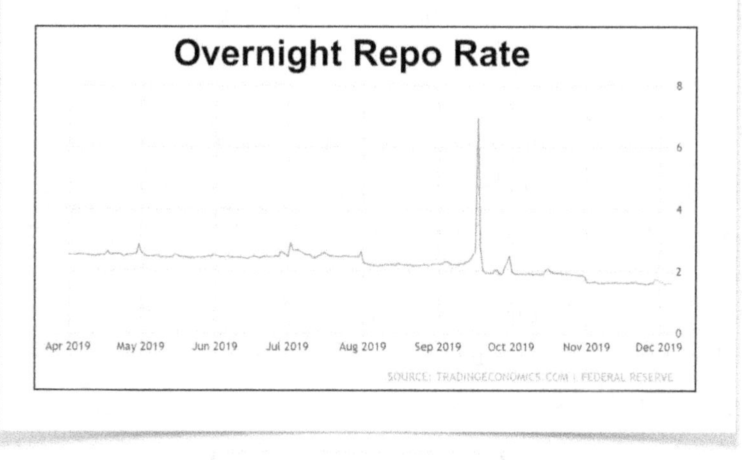

Spike in Repo Rates 2019

When it does break there will be chaos, and in the ensuing chaos it will be easy for populations to be persuaded by their governments that they have the perfect solution ready and waiting for them. Perhaps the governments will offer a new currency coin based on their own centrally controlled blockchain, offered with the promise of even more funding for the NHS, pensions, and welfare (even though these promises are increasingly fraudulent). Will people see the trap?

More money will not solve the problem of the deterioration of these services, when the quality of the money they rely on is now meaningless.

Instead, individuals and businesses can start to move to a world where they choose to exchange value with Bitcoin, circumventing the dishonesty of governments and finally starting to rebuild a system that is based on truth and fairness again. Yes, welfare services will require a different strategy, but with sound money, whatever is created will be built on firmer foundations and less likely to deteriorate with the passage of time.

In the meltdown and all the other distracting misinformation and noise, it is understandable that the majority will be inclined to trust what is being sold to them by their governments. Do they understand the danger they are in? Do they know they have the ability to make a different choice? I hope I have been able to show you here that they do, despite the likely future efforts of those in authority to steer them away from that choice.

The convenience of Bitcoin is perfect for our modern world, and the software has features that prevent its qualities as a sound form of money from being corrupted.

There is still a danger that widespread data collection and analysis through blockchain technology could allow those with superior resources to predict and manipulate others' behaviors. However, even if they do have access to this data, their ability to be exploitative will be more limited if society has a decentralized sound monetary system to rely on.

It is important that efforts continue to be made to implement the privacy features that are currently being designed for Bitcoin's base layer, although a balance will need to be maintained—these software upgrades will need to be watched carefully to ensure that no backdoor mechanisms are allowed in that could lead to the problems I have previously outlined.

There are other blockchains that are purely designed for privacy, but they don't have the network effects of Bitcoin right now, and there is a danger that these privacy coins could take us too far in the other direction, becoming the means by which secret societies continue to operate. These privacy coins may have an important part to play in the future, but that is difficult to predict. Also, if one of these privacy coins develops a particular feature that is popular, Bitcoin can be adapted to adopt it. On this basis most of the other cryptocurrencies are potentially redundant, but they are good sandboxes for exploring new ideas.

By taking the power away from governments to control the money supply, it will no longer be possible for large corporations and monopolies to operate with unfair advantages, in terms of interest rates and tax breaks, that disadvantage the rest of society. It will also render financial speculators obsolete. No longer will people be able to get rich doing things that have no intrinsic benefit to society or others. Freedom from these constraints, and the reduction in the expense of governance and wars, will allow humanity to prosper like never before.

At the moment our existing financial system appears destined to enter a catastrophic failure that can't be fixed, one that has potentially been pre-planned for decades.

Perhaps "they" knew that this would happen to the financial system all along. Maybe "they" had their own digital currencies planned, with a specific timeline in place. Maybe what they didn't plan for was the invention of a decentralized alternative, released to the public anonymously. An invention they could not foresee, that scuppered all their plans.

Bitcoin.

Those in power may be working to create and distribute corporate and government coins on their own centralized blockchains, but if the global population wakes up to the virtues of Bitcoin, their corporate and government coins will fail, because no one will want to use them. When this happens, those now in control are most likely to turn their skills to destroying Bitcoin.

They are trying this already. The introduction of exchange-traded funds has been used for decades to suppress the price of gold to prevent people from realizing what is happening to their currencies. The US government has already admitted that it deliberately brought down the price of Bitcoin with their new futures trading funds, when it was rising exponentially at the end of 2017.[9]

For a while they may be able to continue with this.

The trouble is that, unlike gold, it is easier for people to keep bitcoin in their own possession on their own hardware wallets, or even by remembering a string of simple words in their heads!

In a hyperinflationary crisis, the mechanisms of price control that are suppressing Bitcoin right now will break. The value of Bitcoin will take off like a rocket. Decentralized exchanges will finally facilitate fair pricing around the world.

As chaos unfolds in the economy, what will you do? For myself, as the illusion of minimal inflation continues, I will keep using the fiat currency I am paid for the goods and services I wish to purchase. At

---

9   https://www.coindesk.com/trump-administration-popped-2017-bitcoin-bubble-ex-cftc-chair-says

any opportunity, though, I will happily accept Bitcoin as a form of payment for services I provide. These offers are rare at the moment, but I know exactly what to do when things start to change.

As more and more people opt for this, businesses and individuals will increasingly choose to exchange their skills and services for direct bitcoin payments, but nothing else.

At this time those on the ground that are still able to conduct business independently can request bitcoin in exchange for their goods and services. Those businesses will become stronger and stronger. As others watch the prosperity of these businesses, they will eventually follow and do the same.

It will become a virtuous feedback loop, because the prosperity of those who choose independence, in comparison to those who do not, will be unmistakable. This is what will facilitate the end of the old ways.

From the perspective of many, we live in unfortunate times. Realizing the truth is depressing. In spite of it all, though, there are honorable people that fight the good fight. Many don't even realize their contributions and fail to understand how deeply we should appreciate them. It is thanks to these people that even now humanity lives to fight another day.

One by one, as the truth becomes evident, more people will accept the opportunity that is being presented to them: to take back their power and choose to accept a world where sound money is the basis of exchange. In this way society can return to a world based on the truth, rather than lies, and we can all recover our mental and physical health again.

Until this time, those of us who understand the current situation, can choose to support the network by investing resources in supporting it and spreading the word—perhaps even by sharing and reviewing this book—so that others can learn more about the bigger issues involved with this new technology. Every effort helps, no matter how small, so that gradually, step by step, we can help lead the way into a new world.

There are many of us who now understand that we create our own reality. To achieve this we need to know where to focus our attention. Stories and imagery help to direct our imagination and stimulate our thoughts on where we would like our journey to end. In this spirit I share with you a quote from the Greek poet Hesiod, who maintains that during the Golden Age,

> Men lived like gods without sorrow of heart, remote and free from toil and grief: miserable age rested not on them; but with legs and arms never failing they made merry with feasting beyond the reach of all devils. When they died, it was as though they were overcome with sleep, and they had all good things; for the fruitful earth unforced bare them fruit abundantly and without stint. They dwelt in ease and peace...

Similarly from the Mahābhārata, one of the two major Sanskrit epics of ancient India,

> Men neither bought nor sold; there were no poor and no rich; there was no need to labour, because all that men required was obtained by the power of will; the chief virtue was the abandonment of all worldly desires. The Krita Yuga was without disease; there was no lessening with the years; there

was no hatred or vanity, or evil thought whatsoever; no sorrow, no fear. All mankind could attain to supreme blessedness.

Now it may be that we have been so brainwashed into believing that we need to trade with each other that reaching this definition of a Golden Age seems impossible right now. Society has become so sick we could not be further from this goal. But all hope is not lost. The Mahābhārata has given us a signpost, a way back to the Golden Age:

> The Indian teachings differentiate the four world ages (Yugas) not according to metals, but according to quality, with *Truth* being the defining feature of the Golden Age.

The invention of the blockchain has its dangers. We need to be mindful of these and protect ourselves against them. But the opportunity we have been given to exchange immutable value with each other, to forge relationships based on truth, is a gift we cannot underestimate.

Because in a world where the truth has decayed,

Bitcoin Fixes This.

SWOTting Bitcoin

BITCOIN GIVES US is the opportunity to trade consistently with each other, without the value of what we are exchanging being lost. In my opinion it will be the most appropriate release valve when traditional methods of finance finally break uncontrollably. But that role isn't necessarily guaranteed.

It is important, before we fully embark on our next path, to consider what the true implications might be of a world based on a sound, digital form of money. It is necessary that we recognize the advantages, but also the risks, as we set out on this new adventure.

As the graduate of a business school, I am familiar with a tool known as SWOT analysis. This is often used by businesses and organizations in order to analyze their plans for the future, and is a method that is designed to assess possible strategies for a new endeavor. I am including here my SWOT analysis of Bitcoin, its role as a payment method for businesses, and its implications on our society for the future, for you to see at a glance.

Strengths

- Software system replicating economic properties of gold,
- Sound form of money,
- Money that operates in sync with natural law,
- Preserves fair exchange,
- Trust protocol,
- Sound business operations,
- Sound operation of society,
- Imbues society with integrity,
- Dynamics of the protocol encourages its adoption,
- Desire for monetary security will encourage adoption,
- No one individual or group is able to control the network,
- Gives small businesses a solid foundation to grow on in the future,
- Supports creativity,
- Rewards innovation,
- Provides business and individual resilience in a hyperinflationary collapse,
- Protection from bank failure,
- Protection from bank confiscation,
- Easy to transport,
- Easy to cross borders,
- Potential to be universally accepted,
- Reduces friction in commerce,
- Protects against fraud,
- Network appears more robust and trustworthy with time,
- Unhacked so far,
- Changes to the protocol challenging to implement,
- Decentralized,
- High proportion of early adopters are libertarians.

Weaknesses

- Learning curve required to implement,
- Time-consuming initially,
- Staff-training required in a business,
- Administrative burden in terms of accounting,
- Administrative burden legally,
- Tax burdens implemented by governments,
- KYC and AML regulations required by governments,
- Technology still relatively new,
- Potentially hackable individual accounts,
- Demonstrably hackable exchanges,
- Competition from other projects diverting developers,
- Challenges with scaling the network,
- Lightning network still relatively new, needs to demonstrate persistent reliability,
- Built on a consensus of beliefs, which could change,
- Those motivated by power and wealth may be early adopters, and the rise of Bitcoin will give these people too much power.,
- Potential for corruption and tyranny, allowing the greatest amount of wealth to be concentrated in the fewest number of hands,
- Those that need it the most may be the last to understand it.

Opportunities

- Somewhere to turn when all else fails,
- Re-establish trust in a monetary system,
- Builds a society based on sound money,
- Builds a fairer society,
- Increases prosperity by unleashing creativity,
- Brings smaller businesses back to life, allows them to thrive,

- Successful small businesses will have a better opportunity to take care of their staff.,
- Positive effects on surrounding community,
- Reduces moral hazards,
- Gives the elderly the opportunity to preserve their savings,
- Undermines the exploitative ability of corporations, banks, and governments,
- Levels the playing field again, not just within countries but across the world,
- Provides resilience to individuals and businesses in an uncertain world,
- Reduces friction within commerce, relieving workers of mundane jobs,
- Potential to re-create society in new and creative ways,
- The most prosperous and innovative have the ability to engage in philanthropy.,
- Retirees less burdened by tax and inflation on their savings,
- Will disrupt existing welfare systems, requiring new and creative ways to solve these problematic situations in society,
- By necessity new boundaries will need to be drawn with welfare, as costs will need to be managed in a completely new way.,
- Opportunity to overthrow tyrannical governments,
- Atomic swaps and decentralized exchanges will disrupt the price manipulations on traditional exchanges.,
- An end to the continuous cycle of wars that can no longer be financed.

Threats

- Government legislation,
- Individual, early-adopter businesses targeted by governments,
- Governments hoodwinking the population by repurposing the technology as a means of control through centralized blockchains,
- Government coins,
- Corporate coins,
- Coins based on Keynesian economics,
- Populations unable or unwilling to adapt to change,
- Rigging of exchanges,
- Price manipulation through "spoof trading"—bidding or offering with intent to cancel before execution,
- Price manipulation through "wash trading"—simultaneously buying and selling, creating misleading and artificial information in the marketplace,
- Exchange-traded funds slowing down adoption by manipulating the price,
- Harm to the environment from miners,
- Could allow for unequal knowledge distribution,
- Elite utopia,
- Mark of the Beast/Apocalyptic dystopia,
- Corruption, silent takeover, or backdoors into the technology.

ACKNOWLEDGMENTS

EVERY BOOK IS a successful collaboration with many people, not just the sole efforts of the author, so I would like to take the opportunity here to thank those who have helped me with this endeavor. Firstly I would like to thank my fantastic editor Jeff Shreve who with his intelligent and thoughtful comments encouraged me to explain things I didn't realize I needed to explain. His diligence and efficiency also helped me to publish this book in a timely fashion. Also, my proofreader Kerin Forsyth, who helped to finalize the finishing touches.

I would also like to thank the designer of my book cover—Ariel of 100 Covers, who patiently responded to numerous requests to alter the design of the cover until I felt it was just right. I also want to acknowledge Cherub, Cory, and Wallace for managing the production of the book and its interior design.

Special thanks go to my beta readers—Julie Stone, Nick Gregory, Kirsty Gordon, and Kimberly Byrd—for their thoughtful feedback on the initial drafts of this book.

I would also like to thank my writing coach Sloane Ketcham and the team at the Self-Publishing School for their skill in coaching me on how best to manifest this book.

Thanks also go to my friends Thushanti Rajah, Sylwia & Naran Rathod, Jen Watson, and Amy Schofield for their kind encouragement and patience while I bored them with everything I know on Bitcoin!

I would also like to thank Nind, whose friendship introduced me to the Bitcoin community, and Thomas Hunt (MadBitcoins) of the World Crypto Network, whose interview with me on his YouTube channel took my professional journey with Bitcoin to the next level.

Finally, I would like to thank my parents: my mother for teaching me to think and not accept the world at face value, and my father for teaching me to be independent and, when young, to realize that girls are capable of anything!

My last thank-you goes to my daughter Bethany, whose affection and cuddles keep me going every day!

ABOUT THE AUTHOR

VICTORIA COLLETTE JONES is an award winning dentist, who has worked in the dental industry for over twenty years.

She has had a range of involvement in different public- and private-sector markets, from small family-owned practices to large corporate chains, from local co-operatives to international institutions. She also spent ten years starting up and building her own dental establishment into a profitable enterprise in the private sector, and successfully sold it in 2017. As a result she has extensive experience in varied business environments.

Victoria has also earned an MBA from the University of Nottingham and is interested in the world of commerce and economics, including new payment methods and the ways in which these will influence and profoundly affect our future.

Her familiarization with Bitcoin came in 2016 when she introduced Bitcoin as a payment method into her own business. Victoria now works as a Bitcoin advocate, supporting individuals and businesses that are similarly interested in adopting Bitcoin as a payment method. You can learn more about her and her work at www.satoshispage.com.

Thank You For Reading My Book!

Can You Help?

I really appreciate all of your feedback, and I love hearing what you have to say. I need your input to make the next version of this book, and my future books, better.

Please leave me an honest review on Amazon letting me know what you thought of the book.

Thanks so much!

Victoria Collette Jones